MEASURABLE RESULTS:

Stop Wasting Money and Start Seeing Growth Today

JOHN ARNOTT

TABLE OF CONTENTS

Preface 1

Chapter 1: Introduction 3

Chapter 2: Presence: What Is It? 9

Chapter 3: Presence: How to Make Yours Work for You 17

Chapter 4: Presence: How to Measure Your Results 41

Chapter 5: Leads: What Are They? 53

Chapter 6: Leads: How to Make Them Work for You 61

Chapter 7: Leads: How to Measure Success 79

Chapter 8: Nurture: What Is It? 95

Chapter 9: Nurture: How to Do It 103

Chapter 10: Nurture: How to Measure Success 117

Chapter 11: Reputation Management:
           The Power of Word-of-Mouth 127

Chapter 12: Building Your Online Community 143

Chapter 13: Summary: Measuring the Results
           of Your Marketing Spend 153

PREFACE

If you've picked out this book, you're probably a business owner. You're looking for a way to grow your business, and you know marketing is a vital part of that growth path. But there are so many conflicting sources of marketing information out there – how do you know you're not wasting money on ineffective or outdated techniques? After all, marketing changes quickly these days, and it can be hard to keep up.

What you need is a digital marketing plan that gives you results, and the techniques to measure those results. And you've come to the right place. This book will give you the tools to do both of these critical tasks. It will give you a strong grasp on the ins and outs of digital marketing – how to develop your online presence that speaks for your brand, how to find potential customers and nurture them to a sale, and how to build a strong reputation and community around your brand. After all, these technical details are essential – they're the foundations of digital marketing.

But the most important part is learning how to measure your results. Digital marketing provides us with a wealth of data – if you know how to collect and interpret it, you can ensure you're

1

always making the most effective use of your marketing budget. No matter the size of your company and your budget, you want the most results for the lowest cost. And you can only get that if you can measure your marketing results to find what's working.

Why did I write this book? I've been helping businesses like yours thrive through the power of digital marketing for decades. It's my passion – I want to give every business owner the opportunity to succeed.

It's not an easy process – you'll need to bring a few things to this process to ensure success. You'll need an open and curious mind, a willingness to think differently, and an analytical mindset. And a notepad and pen. But the investment of time and thought will pay off in a focused, data-driven plan that works for the unique needs of your business.

A special Thank You to John Arnott, Sr., without whom I could not have completed this project. I would also like to thank my wife, Daisy, for her never-ending support and my mother, Ellen, for supporting me throughout my life. Finally, I would like to thank my sister, Michelle Prince, for her guidance on the writing and publishing process.

Let's get started. I look forward to taking this journey with you.

Chapter 1

INTRODUCTION

They say half of a business's marketing spend is wasted. The trouble is they do not know which half.

Why is this such a big problem? Well, because if you own one of the millions of businesses in the US, you want it to grow and thrive. After all, you didn't just create your business to be all about the bottom line. You believe in what you're offering to your customers, and you're passionate about your work. And you know marketing is key to increasing your sales and reaching the customers who will love your products. But marketing is an area where it can be all too easy to waste your hard-earned money, in both large and small ways. Many avenues of marketing can be both expensive and confusing - how you do know what's right for your business? After all, your business has unique needs - it's not like every other company on the market. So why are there so many one-size-fits-all options out there, when that's the opposite of what you need?

In today's world, a business owner has so many options and so many conflicting sources of advice, so it can be hard to cut through the noise and focus on what's important. It can be overwhelming to research - print media vs social media? The wide variety of search ads? What should your website do - tell everything about your business or just act as a sales portal? Do you need the bells and whistles, or just the basics? It's a lot to take in. That's why you need the right business marketing solutions. And now, these solutions are digital.

The source of your strategic marketing information is important too: of course, a social media company will tell you Instagram is the answer to building your accounting business. And a website company will insist a glossy home page is how your landscaping business will acquire new customers.

But putting an effective marketing plan in place requires cutting through all that noise and all the biased advice to figure out how to reach and sell to your target customers. Otherwise, you're wasting your time and your money.

The Marketing Mistakes Businesses Make

That's because digital marketing is a wide field. And your plan needs to be targeted to your business and your audience – every business is different.

Here's one way to think about it: if you're a company that sells huge, beautiful, handcrafted sailboats, you want to create an ad campaign that appeals to them. But you listen to a suave ad sales executive who sells you a one-size-fits-all marketing plan - billboards as far as the eye can see, and magazine ads galore. The trouble is, he just reuses his usual marketing plan for boat makers, since he's used to marketing pontoon boats that are popular on Midwestern lakes. He puts those billboards up in the middle of Ohio, far from the ocean where your boats are designed to sail, and puts the ads in newspapers in Pittsburgh and St. Paul. These are not the people who are going to buy your boats, and now you've wasted a whole year's valuable marketing spend on trying to sell ocean-going ships to people who live on a lake. That's because all boat-makers are not alike, and they have different marketing needs.

Another common mistake is ignoring digital marketing altogether, because you don't think you need it. This attitude is common among local business owners, but it's still wrong. Maybe you own a cupcake bakery, and you think your local print advertising and your innovative cupcake flavors and lovely storefront are enough to pull in your customers, so you've totally neglected to build an online presence. But how do many, in fact most, people today find things around them? They type "cupcakes near me" into a search engine, and head to the shop with the best reviews after checking out the menu online. If you think the deliciousness of your cupcakes exempts you from having to do any digital marketing, you're missing out on every one of those customers.

Why A Digital Marketing Strategy Can Save You Money and Time

These can sound like far-fetched examples, but they illustrate a real and very serious principle. You're wasting your marketing dollars and stunting your company's growth if you don't have a strong, targeted, and very thoughtful digital marketing plan in place for your business.

That means more than just imagining what you want your ad campaigns to look like - a very common mistake. Too much time spent imagining a catchy slogan and elaborate ads can actually waste both your time and your money, if you're not starting from the right place.

And where is the right place to begin? It means digging deeper into each of the three main components of digital marketing: how to create a friendly and useful online presence, how to get real leads and convert them into actual sales, and how to continue to build relationships with each customer until you've built a loyal customer base who returns to buy your product again and again.

Does this sound overwhelming? I promise it's not, though it does require time, strategy, and reflection. But that investment will pay off - you can spend less on marketing campaigns and get more customers from your efforts, because you'll be reaching the right audience at the right time. In the end, that's really what successful digital marketing is all about.

Even if your business is generating a positive return on investment (ROI) using traditional advertising platforms, you can boost your ROI with digital marketing. Digital marketing generates 24% higher conversions than traditional advertising. Of course, this shouldn't come as a surprise to anyone who's used digital marketing.

You can make small changes to your campaigns to improve conversions and capture more sales. Perhaps this is why so many business owners are shifting their budgets away from traditional advertising and towards digital marketing services.

What Will This Book Cover?

In the following chapters, you'll learn about the three key components of a digital marketing plan - presence, leads, and nurture - and how to implement and measure the success of each step.

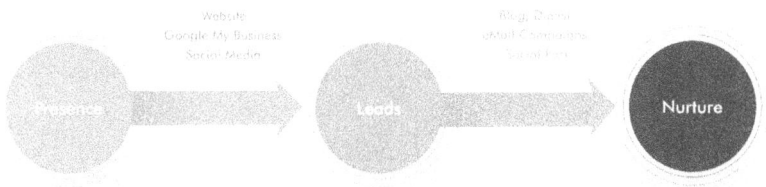

But more than just the steps of successful digital marketing, I'm really here to tell you how to market your business effectively, with the budget you have, and without any unneeded waste. Because here's the big secret of digital marketing: with a strategic plan in place, you don't need to spend huge amounts of money to find success. In fact, it can be one of the most effective and least expensive ways to build your business and grow your customer base, if you're willing to put in the time and thoughtfulness needed.

That's because so much of our everyday lives are online these days - the web and social media are where people find experts to help them, reviews to scout out great local businesses, help with their problems, and communities that connect them. Meeting your customers where they are, with a presence and content that speaks to them, and a community and voice that engages them, can be incredibly effective when it's done well. And that's what I'll show you in this book - how to do exactly that.

Exercise 1: Who and Why

Let's start with an exercise to get you thinking: what's the story of what your business does? I don't mean how you started or a list of products you produce. Write down what the problem is that your customers are having (a hat company serves people who have cold heads or love millinery), and how you solve that and make their lives a little or a lot better. This is where your whole digital marketing strategy will come from - why does your business exist? What need did it grow out of? What problems are you trying to solve?

_____

_____

_____

_____

_____

_____

_____

Chapter 2:

PRESENCE: WHAT IS IT?

What is Presence?

Presence

Website
Google My Business
Social Media

When I talk about presence in digital marketing, I mean the way your business presents itself online. No matter what kind of business you own, you need some form of online presence. It is the first impression of your business that almost all of your customers will have, and we all know how strongly first impressions stay with us. That makes it critically important to get it just right.

Regardless of the industry in which your business operates, your target audience probably uses the Internet daily. 80% of consumers use the Internet to research information about a business's products and services.

If you don't maintain a strong and active presence on the Internet, which is typically achieved through digital marketing, those prospects will likely choose one of your competitors instead — and that's something no business owner wants to see happen.

Even if you're a physical business, like a local tire sales company, customers have to be able to find you online when they're in their driveway, staring at the deflated tire on their Toyota and frantically googling "tire repair near me". Online search is the new Yellow Pages. And without an online presence, you won't be able to reap the many benefits of digital marketing.

The Three Most Important Elements of Presence:

A Clean, Professional Website

This is your digital storefront. You wouldn't expect customers to stay long in a dusty, dimly-lit, messy shop, so the same goes for your online presence. Your website might be the first thing they find about you. If you're pouring money into ads and social media, but your website is old and clunky and unfriendly to use, those marketing dollars are going to waste. Creating a website that enhances your online presence isn't about spending lots of money on fancy features and flashy design - it's all about the story you're telling on it. More on that in the next chapter.

This is the most important element for a simple reason - it's where your customers will ultimately land through whatever digital marketing device takes them there. Your social ads, your email campaigns, your Google reviews - they will end up here. And it's usually on your website that your prospects will become a sale, and a customer. Make very sure that journey is simple, easy, and friendly for them, and they'll reward you with their business.

Customer Reviews

Customers also search frequently for online reviews (in 2018, over 86% of customers read reviews for local businesses), so it's important to have some sort of review page set up. This could be a Google My Business account, which is best for brick-and-mortar businesses. Or it could be a custom paid tool if you're a firm that operates without a physical location (like a mobile catering business). But having this set up is worth the small investment in time it will take to make sure you're easy to find for your potential clients. As your reviews increase over time, you'll find more customers through the power of reputation alone. Ensuring you have a way of getting reviews from your customers and highlighting the best ones will repay your investment of time with a cost savings.

Active Social Media

There are billions of people actively using social media today. That number has done nothing but grow for the past decade, and it isn't showing any sign of stopping. Whatever your product or service, there's no doubt that your target audience is using social media. This makes using a social media platform a must.

Social media is a great place to post content that your target audience is interested in. You can educate prospective customers, engage them on an emotional level, and prove the value of what you're offering. Content posted on social media has the added advantage of being easily shared. Your content can potentially go viral and reach massive numbers of people!

Social media gives your business a friendly voice and an active voice to your customers and leads. Today, customers aren't just looking to buy a product - they want to patronize companies that have a voice and a perspective, that share their values, and that they feel they can trust. The beauty of social media is that it provides you with a way to make this connection to your target customer base.

You also need to make sure you're active and visible on the social media platform that makes the most sense for you. Choose LinkedIn for professional services, Instagram for anything visually-based, and Facebook for most consumer-focused businesses. Don't forget the more niche ones like Yelp, Houzz, and Angie's List.

How to Help Customers Find You

Now that I've covered why it's important to build an enticing and user-friendly online presence, it's time for the next step: how do you make sure your customers can find you? This is where one of the biggest heroes of digital marketing comes in: Search Engine Optimization (SEO).

With SEO, you ensure that your website is designed to be found easily by search engines. It can get technical (maybe you've tried to dive into this yourself and come out confused), but it's really the result of a few simple steps. Ensuring you have a solid SEO strategy makes sure that customers can find your site easily. Over time, it will also contribute to higher organic traffic coming to your website - potential customers searching for a product like the one you sell, or a service like the one you offer. This is the best kind of marketing payoff, because you're not paying for those search results. They're a natural outcome of the easy-to-use and helpful website you've created, not expensive ongoing ad campaigns.

The Basics of SEO – It Starts with the Website

If you've started to try to tackle SEO by yourself before, you know there's a lot of confusing and often contradictory advice out there. This confusion can be compounded because Google has been continuously tweaking its algorithm over the years. When SEO first arrived on the scene as a way to grow websites and get traffic, the strategy mostly consisted of getting as many keywords as possible onto each page, regardless of their grammatical correctness or natural flow. But those days are long gone. Google now ranks sites by a huge range of factors, but what you really need to know is this: it gauges how much time people are spending on your site, if they're finding the content on it helpful for their needs, and if other sites recognize yours as an industry authority.

This means there are a couple of key factors to consider when thinking about your SEO strategy. The overall user experience of the site - is it easy to navigate, and to find the information your readers want? Do the pages load reasonably quickly? Does your site look as good on a mobile device as on a desktop computer? If your visitors find your site clunky, confusing, or unhelpful, they'll leave quickly, and Google will measure that (it's called the bounce rate). If they stay, read the whole article they came in for, and start exploring the other areas of your site, Google notes that your site is helpful and will boost your search ranking so others can find you easily.

It's not just about site design, though that's important - it's also really, really critical to have a thoughtful and engaging content strategy. I can't stress this enough. It can't just be good content, though that's important, obviously, but it also needs to speak to your target audience - and cover their needs. If your content is too general or too bland, you won't engage with the right people - the ones who are actually looking for what you're selling.

Let's look at two basic examples. If you're selling retirement planning services to high-net-worth individuals in New York, the people you want to reach are wealthy, over 55, and living in New York. If you're selling a financial advisory service to entrepreneurs and small business owners in California, your potential customers are probably younger, less wealthy, and live on the other side of the country.

Even though both of the above examples are of businesses offering financial services in the United States, their target audiences are very different.

The best marketing avenues for reaching each type of customer are different as well. For instance, younger people tend to access information almost exclusively online, rendering print advertising ineffective. Older generations, on the other hand, may prefer print. The location difference between these two types of customers is also relevant. As a result, they will respond to different cultural references and they are operating in different time zones.

Content marketing isn't just about creating content for the sake of content. It's to enhance your online presence, establish you as an authority, and engage your customers enough to keep them coming back.

Presence is Many Pieces Working Together

You'll notice this sounds very similar to why social media is important too - that's because creating your online presence is not just a series of discrete steps. It's one big living organism working together, each part helping the other to succeed. Your social media shares your content, which drives customers to your website, which is easy to find on Google because of your thoughtful SEO strategy. Each piece contributes to the success of the others, so don't think that you can just focus on one area alone. For maximum results, incorporate them all in a way that speaks to your target audience.

Exercise 2:

Take a hard look at your current online presence for your business. What's working, and what needs some small or serious improvements? Maybe your website is outdated, or the information on it is old (this is one of the most common problems I see!). Maybe you don't have a single social media account for your business yet, or you haven't set up a Google My Business reviews page. With the story of your business that you identified in the last exercise in mind, take the areas in need of improvement and look at them through the eyes of your customers. Does your total online presence speak to their needs and desires? Why or why not? Make sure to take notes for yourself, as we'll use them in the next section.

_____

_____

_____

_____

_____

_____

_____

_____

_____

Chapter 3

PRESENCE: HOW TO MAKE YOURS WORK FOR YOU

Presence

Website
Google My Business
Social Media

So now that you know what presence is, and why it's essential to an effective and efficient marketing plan, how can you go about creating a robust online presence?

There are several elements you need to perfect in order to make your online presence professional and welcoming to your prospective customers. The overall plan is to go step-by-step, creating each building block one at a time until you have not just one good element, but a series of whole strong and interwoven online ways to engage your potential customers. Without this, any marketing efforts you make will be wasted - at best, not as efficient as they could be, and at worst, just an endless stream of money flowing out with no return at all.

Define Your Target Audience

But first, you have to decide who you're speaking to. Defining your target audience is key to ensuring you're not wasting money on your marketing efforts. After all, you could spend a huge amount of money trying to reach everyone in the U.S., or you could figure out where your ideal customers are and focus on reaching them there. Which effort do you think is more cost-effective and also leads to more sales? So, decide who you're speaking to with your online presence before you create or tweak anything.

Tips for Defining Your Target Audience

Look to Existing Customers

Not sure where to look for the kind of person interested in buying your product? Start with the people who are already using it. Identifying the characteristics of your current customer base will give you criteria for targeting more people who fall into similar categories. The number of data points you can collect from existing customers will depend on how they connect with your business. To make the information usable, you can compile it into a database that you can use to track averages.

For those involved in B2B sales, the data points you collect will be a little bit different. Relevant information may include the size of the businesses buying your product and the titles of the people making the buying decisions. Hence, an awareness of the roles of the people you need to connect with will be key in informing how you connect with potential clients.

Check Your Social Media Analytics

One of the many advantages of having an online presence is that potential customers can interact with your business on their own terms. It means your business can develop a relationship with potential clients even if they haven't purchased your product yet. Paying attention to and understanding social media analytics will help your business form an effective social media voice. This can be the engagement count on your Instagram or Facebook page - be sure to set up a business account as opposed to a personal one on social media sites where that's an option, as that will give you access to more advanced analytics than just the number of likes.

Consider How You Communicate Value

Any highly effective marketer frequently makes the distinction between a product's features and its benefits. The features of your product or service may be very impressive and it may be obvious to you how they create value. But to best connect with customers, they need to be rephrased. Where a product's features are what the product can do, the benefits are what the product can do for the consumer.

Defining the benefits of your product can help you in defining your target audience. Who are the people interested in the benefits you can offer them? For example, if you provide healthcare services, your features might be, "Fully bilingual staff specializing in geriatric care." So, to rephrase this as a benefit, "We speak your language and understand your needs." Examining your value proposition this way can lead you to the people who make up your target audience. In this example, the target audience could be made up of elderly first or second-generation immigrants.

How to Use Your Target Audience

Developing and honing in on your target audience is the first step, but knowing what to do with it is equally important. Here are some tips to keep in mind when developing your marketing strategy.

Target Market Statements

The value of a target market statement is that it can be used to focus and guide your marketing endeavors. It takes the most essential information from your audience and compacts it into a useable statement. For the healthcare provider that provides bilingual geriatrics care in southern California, it might be, "For Spanish-speaking residents of the County of San Diego aged 65 and up who have strong family ties, this healthcare service offers personal, specialized care that provides the peace of mind that comes with being understood and cared for like family."

It's up to you to determine which information is most relevant. If you offer a product or service that can be purchased online, maybe the location of your audience isn't as important as their profession. If you offer multiple products or services, it might be necessary to create several target market statements.

Creating Your Website - The Online Home of Your Business

As I discussed in the last chapter, your strong online presence begins with a professional, inviting, user-friendly website. This is because it's where all the traffic you're trying to bring in will end up. It's the center of your digital marketing efforts. Get this right before you invest any time or money into any other areas of your online presence.

A website homepage can make or break a business. For a homepage to be effective, it must:

- Look good
- Effectively present the product or service it offers
- Encourage the potential customer to buy

Five Elements Every Homepage Must Have

1. Hero Image

As soon as a customer clicks your website, they should see a picture or video that depicts an ideal customer, known as a hero image. This image of a happy customer encourages the customer to buy from you.

Make sure your hero image reflects your primary target demographic. Beacon Wealth's homepage makes excellent use of a hero image, portraying a smiling couple who appear to be in their fifties or sixties, placing them neatly in the business's target demographic.

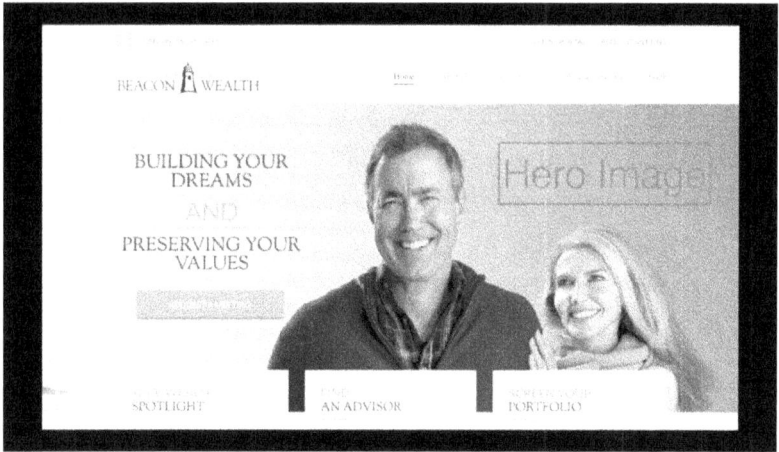

Your homepage should also feature three testimonials. These should be praise for your business from more happy customers. The number of testimonials is very important. Only having one or two may lead viewers to suspect you do not have many satisfied customers to draw from. Having an excessive number of testimonials, on the other hand, makes you look unfocused and overbearing.

Placing exactly three testimonials on your page gives the impression of confidence and authority. The placement of these testimonials within the page may vary. One design method is to place the testimonials in a simple row. Many companies, such as

Keap, use this format. Another way to format your testimonials is to intersperse them throughout your copy, as renowned speaker and author Michael Hyatt does on his site.

2. Call to Action

As with all forms of digital marketing, calls to action are the keys to success with your business's website.

There are two types of calls to action: direct and transitional.

A direct call to action invites the customer to purchase immediately. The most easily recognizable direct call to action is, "Buy now."

In contrast, a transitional call to action is an attempt to get the customer to learn more about your good or service, usually by giving you their contact information. It could say, "Create a free profile," or, "Download this free PDF." Companies use transitional calls to action to move the customer toward a direct call to action. If a customer declines your direct call, you should redirect them to another transitional call. Calls to action should display in the most valuable real estate on your homepage.

The single most important place to put a call to action is the top right corner of your homepage. Customers' eyes are naturally drawn to this area, so you should keep it uncluttered and emphasize your call to action. For most businesses, this should be a direct call. However, for some, such as those with extensive onboarding processes for new customers, a transitional call may be preferable.

Keap, for example, is a software company whose program, although extremely useful, is also very complex, so their homepage features only transitional calls to action. Someone who downloaded the program and jumped right in without any training or explanation would find themselves lost, so all of the calls to action on their homepage lead the customer to more information about the product.

Another business that places a transitional call to action in the upper right-hand corner of their page is Domino's Pizza. One would expect Domino's to have a direct call to action – "order now" – in this area, as pizza is fairly easy to understand. Instead, they have an invitation to create a "Pizza Profile." At first, this seems like a bad marketing decision. As a general rule, any business that can place a direct call here should do so. Domino's, however, makes up for this with a clever strategy.

Every customer with a Pizza Profile will receive an email shortly before their local NFL team kicks off asking them if they want to order a pizza. With the push of just one button, these customers can get their favorite pizza delivered just in time to watch the game. Furthermore, the call to action itself is carefully worded. It doesn't simply say, "Create a Pizza Profile," or, "Click here to get started." It says, "Don't have a Pizza Profile? Create one." This text suggests the reader ought to have a profile and is missing out by not having one.

It is also worth noting the homepage is not lacking in direct calls to action. After opening the page, the customer can see no fewer than five buttons to click to order pizza.

Another prime real estate location on your page is the center of the page above the fold, which remains visible when the reader scrolls down. This area is an excellent place to put a phone number, especially if your target demographic consists largely of older customers. People who are uncomfortable using the Internet will be much more likely to do business with you if they can quickly find a way to contact you offline.

When designing your website, feel free to try out different calls to action. Direct calls to action are often the most effective, but transitional calls can also be great marketing tools.

3. *Three-Step Plan*

No matter how complicated your product or service is, you must present your customers with a three-step plan on your homepage. A short, concise plan of action will establish your brand as an authority in customers' minds.

It is tempting to go into great detail about your business in this plan because you want the customer to know about everything you offer. Simplicity, however, is the key to the three-step plan. Its purpose is to reassure the client you know what to do and encourage them to learn more.

Take, for example, the company Wello®. The founders built this company around temperature sensing technology to prevent epidemics. Obviously, this gives them a lot to talk about, but they have managed to condense a description of their services into a short and sweet three-step plan.

SCHEDULE A CONSULTATION	GET YOUR ACTION PLAN	START USING YOUR WELLOSTATIONX™
Tell us about your facility, your people, your goals, and your needs	Together, we'll combine our data, expertise, and best practices with your goals, people, and company to create a comprehensive plan	Once your WelloStationX™ is up and running, show your patients and staff you care about their safety and well-being

In some cases, a four-step plan may work, but there's a catch. The fourth step should simply describe the benefits of buying your product or service. If you run a pizza shop, and the first three steps of your plan describe the ordering process, the fourth should simply say something like, "Enjoy!"

Some marketers believe the number of steps does not matter, but the truth is a plan with too many steps will leave potential customers bored, confused, or both. Your plan should never have more than four steps. A three-step plan is best because people can easily understand a simple beginning – middle – end structure. Think of it as a very concise way to tell the story of your business.

4. Fresh Content

Another element that needs to display on your page is content. This tip may seem simple, but developers often skip over it during the web design process. Content can take many forms – videos, blog posts, podcasts, etc. On our homepage here at ContentFirst. Marketing, we feature blog posts to give potential customers an idea of the insight and expertise we can offer them.

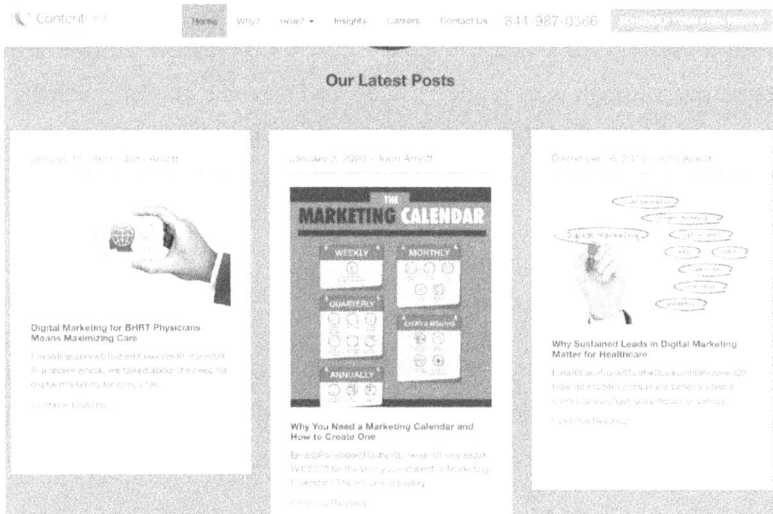

When it's time to go about creating your content, start with reflection - what do your customers and leads want to know about? What is content that would be interesting and useful to them? As a business owner, you're an expert in your industry, so you may be able to write or create this content yourself. If you don't have the time, or writing isn't your strong suit, it can be worthwhile to outsource your content creation to an expert (like at ContentFirst.Marketing). But to get the maximum ROI on the spend associated with content creation, ensure your bloggers are creating thoughtful content that speaks to your customers and readers.

Content and SEO go hand in hand. By creating high-quality content that's interesting and relevant to your target demographic, other sites will want to link to your content naturally, showing the search engines that you're a respected authority in your field. For this reason, it's recommended that you have a sound strategy in place for creating web content. A simple and effective solution is to launch a blog and attach it to your website. You can then schedule posts to be published every couple of days, boosting your site's authority while attracting new backlinks in the process.

5. Marketing Automation

The final key element of a good business homepage is marketing automation. Your homepage should include transitional calls to action that invite the customer to share their email address.

However, simply asking people to sign up for your newsletter or asking for an email address to "stay in touch" will rarely work. One of the best ways to get people onto your email list is to offer them something in exchange.

Michael Hyatt, for example, offers a free eBook to those who subscribe to his email newsletter. Michelle Prince, another successful motivational speaker, offers a free training video in exchange for an email address. Beacon Wealth is a very different business, but it, too, offers something for free. In exchange for your contact information and a list of your biggest investments, they will provide you with a free assessment of your portfolio.

Once you have a potential customer's email address, you can begin sending nurture emails to encourage them to make a purchase. You can perform this task with auto-responder software, which automatically sends emails to those on the list. To maintain a customer's interest without annoying them, send an email as frequently as every day or as rarely as once every week or two. You'll learn much more about email and nurture marketing in future chapters.

Many of the best auto-responders follow a five to seven email structure. First, they send a welcome email sharing basic information about your brand and your mailing list, giving the customer the option to confirm their email address. The next three emails will tell a story or share other useful information to nurture their interest in your company. These emails should be related to each other, but different enough you can use them to segment the customer, using their click-through data to determine what interests them. The information gained from segmenting allows you to tailor your advertising to each customer's needs and wants.

The next email will make an offer. This offer could ask to set up a meeting or consultation, or it could jump straight to "buy now." The next email asks them to subscribe to weekly digest emails, giving them more detailed information about your company, and the seventh makes another offer.

Obviously, you shouldn't stop emailing a customer until you have completed this formula, but you should have enough information to customize your marketing to each.

These five elements are the building blocks of a great homepage. Using them effectively will help you capture your customers' attention, nurture their interest, and boost your sales.

So that's how to create a useful and effective website - the biggest building block in your online presence toolkit. Once that's complete, you can start to build or update the rest of your digital marketing elements.

Create Key SEO Strategy during Presence

Getting your SEO strategy up and running is important. It ensures site will eventually get plenty of organic traffic. Where does your website rank in the search results for its target keyword? If it's buried several pages deep (or not indexed at all), you won't be receiving many visitors. And without visitors, you'll face an uphill battle trying to promote your products or services. It all boils down to search rankings.

The first step in planning an SEO strategy is keyword research. In other words, for which keywords are you hoping to rank? You may already have a general idea of some basic keywords, but you need more information on them, such as search volume, competition, related keywords, etc. Google's Adwords Keyword Planner Tool is an excellent (and free) tool for this purpose. As long as you have an Adwords account, you can use the tool to research keywords for your SEO strategy.

Promote Higher Search Rankings with These Simple Tips.

1. Publish High-Quality Content

Let's first get the most obvious SEO tip out of the way: publish high-quality content on a regular basis. In its guide titled, "Steps to a Google-friendly site," Google says this is the single most important thing webmasters can do. Publishing high-quality content will encourage search engines to crawl your website and to rank it higher in their results.

But what's key for maximum effectiveness in creating content? A purposeful intention and a strong plan. If you create lots of content but it's too broad, too vague, or just not what people are searching for, you'll be expending that time and possibly money for nothing.

2. Keep Your Site Updated

When was the last time you updated your website? Even if it's currently ranking high for its target keyword, you should still update it regularly. Doing so shows Google and other search engines that you are proactive towards maintaining your website. This, in turn, will help you achieve and maintain a high search ranking. Tip: you'll want to include updating your content management system, template/theme, add-ons, and content.

3. Social Signals

Social signals such as Facebook likes and Twitter tweets/retweets will also play a role in your site's search ranking. You can encourage visitors to create these social signals by adding social buttons somewhere on your website. Clicking a Facebook like button that's embedded in a website is easier than logging into your account and liking the page, making this a highly effective form of promotion.

4. Attract Backlinks

Google is constantly tweaking the algorithm it uses to rank websites, by adding new ranking signals while removing or devaluing old ones. With that said, backlinks remain a time-tested ranking signal, with all of the major search engines using them in their ranking algorithms. Rather than manually creating backlinks, however, focus on creating high-quality content that other users and websites want to link to. Tip: when you have links on your page or blog, write out the keywords in the hyperlink, instead of just "here."

5. Mobile Compatibility

If your website isn't compatible on both desktop computers and mobile devices, you could be leaving tons of potential traffic up for grabs. Studies have shown that more people now access the Internet on a smartphone or mobile device than desktops. This means websites which are not mobile-friendly lose up to half of their visitors due to compatibility problems.

Your SEO strategy and content strategy clearly go hand-in-hand. SEO doesn't work right away - it takes a while to see traffic results increase and your rankings grow. For example, The Expo Group, a national exhibitions and events company, first used its SEO research to better understand what its target customers were searching for online. It then viewed how well their competitors were responding. With this intelligence, there SEO strategy included new website content, targeted weekly articles and social media posts to answer prospect's high demand search questions. After six months, organic traffic began to rise. By month nine it had risen from 376 users to 789 users: a 101% jump.

But since it's the best long-term solution for growth, you should begin thinking of and prioritizing it on your site as soon as possible.

Social Media Strategy

Now it's time to start on your social media presence. A strong social presence isn't just for the big companies anymore. Local digital marketing is just as important so potential clients in your area can find you and know what you offer. This is essential because it's how you can talk directly and authentically to your customers and leads. The most important part of creating your social media presence requires initial strategy, in two parts: deciding who you're speaking to and what kind of voice they will respond to.

As you probably know, in today's world there's a huge variety of social media platforms out there. If you try to excel on all of them, you'll be exhausted and out of marketing dollars in no time flat. Getting the most value out of your marketing spend is best achieved by narrowing down exactly who you're trying to reach on social media, and where the optimal platforms are to do this.

For example, if you're selling customized sweatshirts with funny mom memes on them, using TripAdvisor is not going to pay off for you. Your ideal customers are moms – so what social media sites are they using? Instagram is great for visually focused businesses, and Facebook is ideal for local businesses. If you're a business consulting firm, like one of our clients who offers executive leadership solutions for companies who need technology leadership, LinkedIn will reach those high-level business decision makers. Houzz is essential for interior designers.

Once you've figured out who your customers are and what social media platforms they use, you need to figure out how you want to talk to them. This is where you find your social media voice - what will speak to your leads and encourage them to trust and engage with you?

Find Your Social Media Voice

Be sure to find your social media voice – first, think about those target customers I discussed above. How do you want to talk to them?

You might also be wondering why voice is important in social media marketing. Social media is used to create relationships with a person or brand's followers, and the right voice will convey your message in a more personal and meaningful manner.

Speaking in third person isn't going to have a positive impact on your social media followers. Opting for first-person, however, will almost certainly benefit your social media marketing efforts. Of course, perspective is just one of the many elements to consider when choosing your social media voice.

Voice is also important because it reflects your brand as a whole. If you come off as sounding unprofessional, visitors may assume this is indicative of how you handle business, at which point they will be less likely to purchase your products or services.

Now for the million-dollar question: how do I find my brand's voice? There are three key elements: culture, community, and conversation.

Culture consists of traits and characteristics that make your brand stand out from its competitors. Community consists of the way in which a brand's target audience speaks to them (e.g. posting comments on social media, sending private messages, etc.). Lastly, conversation is the content that you wish to post on your social media accounts. By combining culture, community, and conversation, you'll have an easier time identifying the best possible voice for your social media marketing campaigns.

Tips on Using Your Voice in Social Media

– Be consistent with your voice. Once you've chosen a voice and tone, stick with it throughout all of your social media marketing efforts.

– Market your brand as if it were a person.

– Use a personal tone on social media.

– Add adjectives to describe your brand and its respective products and/or services.

– Don't try to force a tone that isn't working.

– Browse through other successful brands to see which style of voice they are using.

Don't Neglect Online Reviews

Google reviews, above all else, are the single most important thing you can do for your business – especially if your business has a physical location and services a local area. When your reviews are tied to your Google My Business page, they are also tied to the map pack, which is something your business can't thrive online without.

When your reviews outnumber those of your competitors, you don't have to spend as many ad dollars to beat them in search results. Google recognizes a more reviewed business as being more credible, more trustworthy, and more important to the user. Hence your local search ranking will improve as planned!

Although Google reviews seem simple enough, they are quite powerful. If you decide to put an emphasis on growing your reviews, there are some tips you'll need to keep in mind.

Regularly Monitor Reviews

An easy way to build a good reputation? Be responsive to your reviews. Designate a team member to respond to reviews once or twice a week and have a set of appropriate responses that can be modified to fit reviews.

Keep the Negativity Offline

Patience and professionalism are key here, and even if someone writes a harsh review, customers will tend to side with the other reviewer and not the business. Do your best to reconcile with negative reviewers offline; this also gives you an opportunity to see where things went wrong and clear up any miscommunication. If you do respond to the negative review in front of the whole world, make sure you say something like, "contact us and we'll be happy to help fix the problem", always keeping communication professional.

Don't Copy and Paste Replies

While it's time-efficient to have a script, you don't want to come off as a robot. Make sure your replies still feel personal.

Watch Comments for Language

Remove hate language, profanity, and other inflammatory statements. While you can't edit a review, I recommend deleting the whole thing if it includes hate speech.

Your online presence is your digital storefront - make sure it's thoughtfully designed and user-friendly before you begin any marketing campaigns. Otherwise, you won't be using your marketing dollars effectively. Think about it in real-life terms: if you have a dingy and outdated store that's poorly lit and poorly organized, you don't start bringing in business by putting up big shiny billboards all over town. You take care of the heart of your business first.

Exercise 3:

Using your notes on examining your overall online presence in the last exercise - where you're doing okay and where you have room for improvement - pick the most critical area and write down 5 steps you can take to quickly improve it. Over time, you'll of course want to address all the shortcomings, but I know you wear a lot of hats as a business owner. You're busy. What will give you the most impact in the shortest time? Maybe it's adding strong call-to-action buttons on every key part of your website, or just setting up a Google My Business profile. A small step now is a big step towards getting measurable results from your existing or future marketing efforts.

_____

_____

_____

_____

_____

_____

_____

_____

_____

Chapter 4

PRESENCE: HOW TO MEASURE YOUR RESULTS

Presence

Website
Google My Business
Social Media

At this point, you've learned all about the importance of having a vibrant and up-to-date digital presence for your business. Your overall presence - your website, social media, blog, and reviews - are working together to create a lively digital hub that your potential customers want to visit and spend time in.

That's great! But how do you know if it's working? Are you getting real results from the expense and time you've put in? That is a key question to ask yourself to ensure you're not wasting your marketing investment.

Here are some ways to measure how successful your online presence is for your business.

Measure Your Website Traffic

One of the biggest ways to measure if your website is working the way you intended is to measure the amount of people who visit it. This is especially important for making sure your SEO strategy is working - it won't happen immediately, but you want to see a steady upward trend of visits and sessions. Depending on your content strategy, it will likely take about 9-12 months for your SEO results to show up fully, so keep that in mind.

Operating in the digital realm affords businesses some unique advantages. One of these is the availability of useful data. Data such as website behavior and download history can be key in helping you better understand your customers' wants and needs.

The best way to measure your website traffic growth and other data is through your Google Analytics account. If you don't already have one, this is a must! It will give you rich data on how many people visit your site, the pages they visit, and how long they stay. Best of all, it's free.

Google Analytics will also give you the most important piece of information you need to know if your online presence is going to help you grow: the profile of the people who visit your site. In the last chapter, I talked about the importance of developing your target customer - the specifics of the people who will benefit from what you're offering.

You want your business to be as successful as possible, and that means reaching as many people as possible, right? Not necessarily. A core part of any successful marketing campaign is speaking to your target audience.

Directing your marketing efforts at specific groups of people will dramatically increase their efficiency. And it's a pretty straight-forward concept. Your marketing team's time and energy will see a higher return when focused on people who actually want to buy your products or enlist your service.

Digging into the Google Analytics data on who is visiting your site will tell you if you're reaching that target audience or not. If your product is marketing services for small businesses in California, and your website is mostly being visited by retirees in Arizona, even if your traffic is high, it isn't effective. This data will tell you if you need to refocus your SEO or content creation strategy and will prevent you from wasting your marketing dollars as we move on to the next step of lead generation.

There are a few other helpful data points to measure as well in your quest for effective marketing:

Keywords

It's important to research relevant keywords to include in your content. Google looks for keywords and keyword phrases to help steer users toward the best possible search results. It's best to focus on longtail keywords to rank higher. That's because searchers - with a strong intent to find services - generally need 4 to 5 words in length. Another benefit: these searches generally convert more frequently when they find a clear match online.

Keep an eye via Google Search Console (another free and data-rich tool) to see how you rank for the keywords you're focusing on. You'll want to see that trending upwards over time too - that will tell you if your keyword strategy is working or not.

Search Queries

Arguably, one of the most powerful metrics of Google Analytics is the ability to track search queries. In other words, you can find out which keywords a visitor searched for to find your website. With this information on hand, you can optimize your website to rank higher for those keywords, resulting in even more traffic to your website. Simply choose Acquisition > Search Engine Optimization > Queries. Keep in mind that data here is about 2 days old, meaning you won't see any major improvements after making changes to your website for at least a couple of days.

Dwell Time

This is the amount of time a website visitor spends on a page, and the longer the better. Pages with higher average dwell times rank higher on Google search results. A high dwell time also means your content is successfully connecting with your visitors - they're really engaging with the page and the information on it. That's exactly the result you're looking for. The average dwell time of a top-10 Google result is 3 minutes and 10 seconds. So, crafting relevant and high-quality content is essential.

Bounce Rate

Another key performance metric that can be tracked using Google Analytics is bounce rate. Bounce rate is described as the percentage of visitors — either page-specific or site-wide — who leave without accessing a second page on the site. A bounce can be triggered when the visitor clicks the back button in their browser; closes their web browser, clicks on an external link, or remains idle for a given period of time.

The bounce rate is important to gauge message quality. For example, A SW healthcare product manufacture, introducing a new product on Facebook, had great success. Its referral traffic spiked from 8% to 44% of total traffic – up 1100 users – in just 5 weeks. Wow! Unfortunately, when the Facebook users reached the site, 90% bounced in the first minute. Why? The ad promise and site message didn't match. The reader became confused and a "confused mind never buys".

Generally speaking, you want to optimize your site for a low bounce rate. This can be done by publishing high-quality content that's relevant to your target demographic, and monitoring weekly.

Click-Through Rate (CTR)

How often do people click on your link? Pages with higher CTRs get ranked higher in Google search results. A page with a title and meta description that are optimized with keywords will generate more clicks. Another way to attract more clicks is to include numbers and emotional hooks in a page title.

Mobile Visits

What percentage of your site's visitors are using a mobile device? Using Google Analytics, you can learn this and more to determine whether or not you need a mobile-friendly design change. After logging into your GA account, choose Audience > Mobile > Overview, at which point you'll see a list of your mobile visitors, along with their device type, pages per session, average time spent per session, and more. If you have a significant number of mobile visitors who are leaving your site after just a couple of seconds, it could be indicative of a more serious underlying problem, such as broken functionality for mobile users.

New vs. Returning Visitors

The benefits of using Google Analytics don't end there. This versatile tool can also track your ratio of new vs. returning visitors. Why is this important? Well, if the vast majority of your site's visitors are "new," there's probably some problem or reason that's preventing them from returning. Perhaps the content isn't relevant to their needs, or maybe there's a broken button on your website that you don't know about. Webmasters should optimize their websites to maintain a high percentage of returning visitors.

Geo Location

Last but not least, you can identify the location of your website's visitors via Google Analytics. From the Audience > Geo >

Location tab, you can see where your visitors are coming from. If most of your visitors are located here in the U.S., you should in turn focus your marketing efforts on U.S. traffic. But if more visitors are coming from Canada or the U.K., you should focus your marketing efforts there to maximize conversions.

Social Media Measurement

To ensure social media is playing an impactful role in your digital marketing strategy, you need to have well-defined, actionable goals. What do you want to get out of your social media plan? Be specific and identify the steps you will take. To increase brand awareness, it's best to focus on creating content that emphasizes your company's personality. Users respond to this type of content more than promotional material. And you can track brand awareness with metrics like number of followers or content views.

Your Content Marketing Results

Content marketing is a powerful inbound marketing technique that involves creating and publishing high-quality content that's relevant to your target audience. This is the kind of content I talked about in the last chapter - thoughtful, insightful, well-written media (most often a blog, but it could be via video or another medium) that speaks to your customers and that you push out on a regular basis.

This doesn't necessarily mean you have to pitch your product or service directly. Rather, you want to produce content that entices prospective customers and clients to engage with your business, which can subsequently lead to sales. In addition to attracting customers and generating sales, content marketing can also build authority and credibility for your business.

But how do you know if your content marketing efforts are helping your business? Here are three ways to track your efforts.

1. Track Sales-Accepted Leads (SAL)

A strong content marketing strategy is sure to attract leads, but how many of those leads follow through the sales funnel? This is where tracking sales-accepted leads (SAL) comes into play. A SAL is a lead produced through your marketing efforts that have been accepted by the sales team. Granted, a SAL isn't necessarily a paying customer (not yet, at least).

You want to track the number of SALs produced through your content, website, and social media to determine whether or not it's having a positive impact on your audience, as well as the overall value of your content. Investing thousands of dollars and 100+ hours into creating a single piece of content may sound wasteful. But if it has attracted 250 SALs since you published the content, it was probably worth the investment.

2. Track Brand Name Mentions

You should also track the brand name mentions generated from your content and social media. The higher your website ranks for its target keywords, the more traffic you'll receive. Traffic that can be used to sell a product or service. But do you know how many people are searching for your brand name in the search engines?

Scouring the Internet for mentions of your brand name by hand is a painstakingly tedious process. So, how are you supposed to track this data? There are dozens of tools and services that business owners can use to monitor mentions of their brand name, one of which is Google Alerts. You can set up a Google Alert for any topic you like, and set up preferences for how often you'd like to receive them, what parts of the world you'd like to focus on, and more. For your business, you could set it up to receive weekly alerts of mentions of your business name in the US if that's relevant, or more frequently if needed.

3. Measure Sentiment

Many business owners and digital marketers overlook the importance of user sentiment in marketing. Sentiment refers to how the audience feels about a particular brand or interaction with the brand. Of course, measuring sentiment from content marketing isn't as easy as tracking unique views or clicks — but you can still do it.

Consider:

– Evaluating comments: look to see what visitors had to say about the content.

– Were they satisfied or even thankful that you published the content?

- How many visitors published negative comments about the article?

- Editing content: control sentiment through regular editing. Just because an existing article or content piece has generated negative sentiment doesn't mean you cannot turn it around into a positive sentiment.

These are just a few of the most important metrics to track about your content.

What Not to Do

There's no better way to understand your site visitors and how they're interacting with your content than by using cold, hard data. That being said, it's easy to get swept up in what the marketing world calls "vanity metrics." They can be misleading and ultimately not indicative of how your brand is performing in the digital sphere. Be wary of these vanity metrics, and try not to get too wrapped up in or spend money on boosting them. That's a great way to waste your marketing dollars quickly.

Twitter Followers

On Twitter, sometimes "following" people is totally random. Plenty of users use Twitter to keep tabs on a variety of interests, but that doesn't necessarily mean they are interested in making a purchase. In fact, they may just want a "follow back" in order to boost their own numbers.

Do This Instead: Look at the number of followers of your direct competitors. Are they more or less? This basis of comparison can help you understand if you can improve your content strategy and where you're already hitting the mark.

Facebook Fans

Same principle applies, as with Twitter followers. Many users will click "Like" on a page, but never or seldom return back.

Do This Instead: A better metric to look at is engagements; who is commenting, sharing, and liking your posts, versus just liking your page. Facebook has a free analytics tool called Facebook Insights where you can monitor your engagement levels.

Blog Views

You're getting a lot of views to your blog — that's great! But blog views don't indicate where your reader came from or where they're headed on your site.

Do This Instead: Monitor bounce rates. Bounce rate is when a visitor visits one page, then does not click further into your site. A high bounce rate is bad because it means visitors leave your site after visiting just one page. Also, look at shares on social sites, as search engines consider shares and tweets in their results.

Constantly Refine Your Strategy

Although conducting a deep-dive into your metrics important, be sure to re-evaluate your efforts, as it can take time to really see whether your methods are working or not.

What is working well and connecting with your customers?

How can you adjust your brand message to better reach the people you want to?

Remember that nothing stays the same forever. The marketing channels your target audience prefers or the language they use can change. The people that make up your target audience might even change. In these cases, you'll need to make changes to your online presence strategy.

Exercise 4:

Dig into your Google Analytics data. Pick three areas where you see room for improvement - it could be a high bounce rate, a low keyword ranking, or maybe you're attracting people who live outside the area you operate in. For each of the three areas, write down one step you can take to improve - whether it's a quick fix or a longer-term solution. This will put you on the path to a refined and effective digital presence strategy before we get to the next chapter.

_____

_____

_____

_____

_____

_____

Chapter 5

LEADS: WHAT ARE THEY?

The middle part of effective marketing - the kind where you're getting results you can measure without wasting money - is focusing on your leads, which are the people who are interested in buying what you're selling.

Especially for B2B (business to business) companies, lead generation sits at the epicenter of your business's growth. Leads, when nurtured well, will turn into sales. Those sales turn into relationships with customers that are loyal to your brand and will refer you to their friends, family, and colleagues.

Lead generation is the beginning of growing and maintaining your business. However, lead generation is a means to an end because the goal is not to just generate leads, it's to generate sales.

I'll talk about how you get them, how you convert them to sales, and how to measure your success.

So, first, what are the most important things to know about leads?

The Two Types of Lead Generation: Quick vs. Sustained

Quick Leads:
Market Your Business Fast, But at a Cost

Many of the benefits of digital marketing can take a while to impact your business's bottom line. If you're looking to get some clients or customers now because your business has bills to pay, you'll want to invest in getting some quick leads. These are fast-acting but also effective because you pay for them – no freebies here.

There are three main kinds of quick leads your business could use as part of your digital marketing plan:

Paid Search Ads

Paid search ads like Google Ads can be a great fit if you sell a product that customers frequently search for. That way, you'll show up quickly at the top of search pages even if your website is brand new. Paid search ads work best for businesses where customer intent is really important – they're already looking for what you're selling. You're not convincing them they need the general product or service, just to choose yours over the next one.

Paid Social Ads

An alternative is paid social ads – basically getting your product in front of prospects who aren't searching for you but might like what you have to offer. With paid social ads (usually ads on Facebook or Instagram), you're looking to increase your brand awareness to a targeted audience.

One of my clients, Complete LandSculpture, saw a big increase in their business despite having a brand-new website by investing in thoughtful paid Facebook ads targeting their market.

To maximize effectiveness, you can combine paid search ads with paid social ads. A prospect searches for a product like yours and is interested enough to click through to your site from a paid search ad, but doesn't immediately make a purchase. Later, when the prospect is on Facebook or Instagram, ads pops up reminding them of their interest in your product and keeping your product top-of-mind.

Paid Display Ads

Finally, paid display ads like the banners on the tops or sides of websites can also be a source of quick leads. Don't just do those without investing in paid search or paid social though, as they're an accessory to those methods, not a good stand-alone.

So if quick business is what you're after, paid search, paid social, and paid display ads are proven routes to a quick boost in sales. This fast approach is one of the many benefits of digital marketing.

Sustained Leads:
Playing the Long Game for Long-Term Growth

To grow your business long-term you will need a sustained digital marketing strategy. Quick leads will only get you so far, and they'll cost you a pretty penny along the way. That cost means they're not an ideal long-term growth strategy.

To build steady growth for the future, you should invest your time into building sustained leads. This means building your website as a respected online presence. And it entails boosting your search rating so your website (not just your ads) appears on the first page of Google or Bing results. It also involves growing your social channels so you have lots of organic social media followers instead of just paid ads. You want to be seen as a trusted expert in your field.

This is a natural by-product of creating excellent targeted content on your site consistently, which raises your SEO ranking naturally. Targeted is the key word here - you're not just trying to attract lots of general traffic with broad, vague content. You want to be creating articles or videos that speak to the needs, concerns, and interests of the people who are most likely to buy your product. That's how you turn traffic into leads, and those leads into sales.

The Three Main Lead Categories

Information Qualified Leads (IQL)

These are when a lead first connects with your business. They have given their contact info in exchange for some piece of valuable content, such as an eBook or free download.

IQLs usually don't know a lot about your business or how you can help them. Following up with an IQL should involve opportunities to learn more about your company. You can do this by offering webinar access, case studies, or a link to your blog.

Marketing Qualified Leads (MQL)

The MQL has interest and has moved passed the stage of IQL. They understand what you're offering and are considering your solution, shown by downloading or interacting with your content.

Here is a tip if you're using an automated system: your sales team should double-check your lead and learn as much about them before moving them on through the sales process. Move your MQL by giving them incentives to take action: maybe a discount, free trial/demo, free consultation, or an estimate.

Sales Qualified Leads (SQL)

The customer is ready to close the sale. They've shown interest in your business, have downloaded your content, have requested a consultation or something similar. They're ready to make a decision. An SQL should be assigned to a specific salesperson, who should then contact the lead directly to work on finalizing a sale.

These techniques will help you save precious time and avoid human error in deciding which leads to pursue. Using objective data to qualify leads will also help you find patterns in your leads and sales. After all, the goal is to improve your marketing strategies further.

Knowing exactly what leads are, and the two main categories of generating them, will help you take your business to the next level. Having a strong understanding of leads helps you prevent waste in your marketing spend - by understanding who you're trying to reach and how to best reach them, you'll become more efficient at a lower cost.

Exercise 5:

Take the list you have of your current leads (this could be your email list, if you don't have a specific leads list), and segment them into the categories above. Is there one area that's lagging - maybe you have a lot of IQLs and only one or two SQLs? Notice the patterns that emerge and which areas need work.

_____

_____

_____

_____

_____

_____

_____

_____

_____

Chapter 6

LEADS: HOW TO MAKE THEM WORK FOR YOU

Leads

Social, Search, Display

So, you know all about the types of leads. But how do you put that knowledge into action? There are so many ways to generate leads and get them into your sales funnel. But a lot of them can cost you huge amounts of marketing dollars, and not all of them have a high ROI. So let's talk about the most efficient and cost-effective ways to make those leads work for you.

Advertising is one of the main solutions, but that covers everything from glossy magazine ads to billboards to website pop-ups. If you're looking for cost-effective marketing, digital ads are the way to go. With the amount of time everyone spends online these days, digital marketing is the best way to reach people easily. But there are three different kinds of online ads to know about, and how they work together.

Search Ads:
How to Make Them Appealing to Your Leads

To say there's a lot of searches performed on Google.com would be an understatement. In an interview with SearchEngineLand, Google revealed that it parses more than 3 billion search queries per day, or 1 trillion per year. This is why search ads, like Google Ads, are one of the most powerful ways to get leads to your website to make a purchase. There's a lot to learn about how to use the powerful tool effectively, but let's start with some definitions.

What is Pay-Per-Click (PPC) Marketing?

It's a kind of digital marketing strategy using pay-per-click ads that shows up on a search results page. To ensure a high return on your investment, you need to plan out your pay-per-click campaign.

A PPC campaign is your ad strategy that involves targeting choices, pricing models, creative messaging, and metrics to track the effectiveness of your ad copy.

Pay-per-click ads (PPC ads) are ad copies that appear in places where your customers search on the web, whether it's Google

Search or Maps. Advertisers pay when the readers click on your ads.

Simply put, you pay for the ad each time someone clicks on the link.

Your PPC ad shows up on a tablet, PC, or smartphone — whatever gadget your potential customer is using for his search query. And it also shows up on the search engine or social media platform where your potential customers go to find information.

Your PPC ad is targeted to the customers who are in your target market. This helps you minimize unqualified leads (or people who don't belong to your target population). Therefore, you increase your online presence when your PPC ad drives your target customer population to your website or social media platform, or gets them to pick up the phone to make an appointment.

You only pay for PPC ads that capture your target audience. So, you could set a cap and adjust your budget as you see fit. You can even analyze what ads are more effective in driving visitors to your website and siphon your resources to run those kinds of PPC ads.

Will Pay-Per-Click Marketing (PPC Marketing) Work for Your Business?

It would if you have a website that can convert a reader to a customer. Essentially, driving traffic to your website is one of the main goals of pay-per-click ads.

What Not to Do with Search Ads

Google Ads can be one of the most powerful marketing tools available for driving people back to your website. If you're not careful, though, it can also be a tremendous money sink. The key to seeing an excellent return on your investment is to understand the foundation of a smart Google Ads strategy, and the first step is recognizing your mistakes.

Many marketers make serious mistakes with their Google Ads campaigns without ever knowing it. Let's look at the five most common ways you might be sabotaging your marketing efforts without realizing it:

Failing to Make Keyword Groups

Google Ads works by targeting keyword searches: whenever someone types in a particular keyword or phrase, your ad appears in the search results. You can target multiple keywords with any given ad in order to capture the attention of more potential shoppers.

Knowing this, many amateur marketers are tempted to stuff as many keywords as possible into one ad. Doing so, however, is a mistake. Remember: your goal is to secure conversions, not simply get eyeballs on your ad. It doesn't matter if thousands of people see your ad if none of them click on it and ultimately make a purchase.

Therefore, your primary objective should always be to tailor the advertisement to the people most likely to take action. To do this, you'll want to build ads around keyword groups. This allows you to create ads that are highly relevant to the keywords targeting them.

For example, imagine that you sold shoes. While you could certainly run a single ad for "Joe Blow's Shoe Store" for every shoe-related search, wouldn't it be much more effective to run different ads for high heels, athletic shoes or children's footwear depending on what the shopper is searching for? Someone looking specifically for high heels may not be immediately tempted by a general shoe store ad, but that same shopper might be very interested in clicking if the ad displayed exactly the type of shoes she wanted to buy.

Knowing your audience and understanding what people are looking for when they make various searches will get you a long way toward building highly-targeted, effective advertisements. Avoid the temptation to take a shotgun approach to marketing; spend a little extra time or money on tailoring ads to your audience. The rewards will be worth it.

Failing to Test Ads

As you gain experience in marketing, you'll quickly discover that one piece of advice comes up again and again: test everything! Testing is the backbone of a successful marketing strategy because it allows you to see whether your ideas are truly effective. No one is psychic, and even the best predictions might turn out wrong. This is why you should never invest too much time, money, or effort into something until you've tested it and proven that it's effective.

When it comes to Google Ads, testing comes in a few forms. The first thing you'll want to do is test the ads themselves to be sure that they're having the appropriate effect. You might think that your ad is brilliant, but if your audience doesn't feel the same way, it won't convert. Try running a split-test where you show two different ads to the same demographic of viewers and record which is the most effective. Keep tweaking your ads and testing them until you see the results you want.

Here's something a lot of people forget to include in their ad copy: A a call to action. This is a huge mistake. You need to make it absolutely clear to your audience what exactly you're expecting them to do after they click the ad. Are they supposed to simply visit the site, or do they need to enter a promo code to get the discount you're advertising? Spell it out in the ad, then test a few different versions of your call-to-action to see which is the most effective.

Another thing you'll want to test is your keyword targeting. It's possible that people are not searching for what you would expect them to search for. If you're not getting the results you want from your campaign, try tweaking your keyword groups to be more inclusive. Do more research as necessary to find the right words or phrases, then test them to be sure you're on the right track.

One thing that many people don't consider is your ad placement. When you buy a Google ad, you'll be given a price range. The more you pay, the higher your ad will be placed in search results. While it may seem like higher is always better, you might be surprised: while high-placing ads get a lot of impressions, the people who see and click them aren't always interested in buying what they've found.

Quite often, these ads are clicked simply by people who are curious or even clicked by mistake. However, if your ad falls further down the page, it's likely that the only people who will seek it out and click on it are those who are interested in buying whatever it is that you have for sale.

With this in mind, experiment with your ad placement. If you find that your ads perform just as well or even better at the third or fourth spot on the page, you can save yourself a hefty chunk of change on your marketing budget.

Not Capturing Repeat Visitors

A Google Ads campaign is great for capturing the attention of new customers, particularly when you need to drive traffic to your site for a special event or promotion. Unless you take steps to keep them, though, your Google Ads campaign will result in, at best, one-time customers or people who just browse through your page but don't take any further action.

Setting up an ad campaign is only half the battle of smart marketing. You also need to be prepared to capture vital information about your visitors so that you can reach out to them in the future. In other words, you need their email addresses.

An email address acts as a tether to your site. Once you have it, you'll be able to entice readers back to your business through well-written email campaigns and special offers. In order to sweeten the deal, you'll need to offer a value exchange to your visitors: people who give you an email address will receive an attractive offer. This is called an engagement offer or a lead magnet and marketing your site without one is never a good idea.

Generate a lead magnet that offers something of value, whether it's a free report, a sample product, or a valuable bundle of coupons. When a person signs up for your mailing list, he'll automatically receive what you're offering.

Not Knowing How to Set a Smart Budget

Marketing is expensive, especially when you're using something as competitive as Google Ads. If you're not careful with your budget, it can quickly get away from you without delivering the results you need.

First, it helps to be realistic with your goals. You are not going to launch a multimillion-dollar company overnight with $500 in Google Ads. You may, however, very successfully drive some traffic toward your site in time for a major sale or offer. When establishing your budget, it helps to keep the parameters of your campaign in mind.

Keeping your ads running indefinitely will drain your wallet faster than it will fill it. Instead, choose a well-defined beginning and end to your campaign and focus your energy on making that single campaign as effective as possible. Later, you can launch another one taking into account what you've learned.

Sending People to the Wrong Page

You want to remove as many barriers as possible between your customer and the sale. This means that once a visitor has clicked your ad, he should land immediately on the product he wants to buy. If he ends up on your home page, he may end up becoming bored or confused and wandering away from your site before he ever gets the chance to buy what he came there for.

Make sure that your ads lead to a page that makes sense and delivers what the visitor is expecting. Depending on the ad, this landing page might be a category page, a specific item listing, or a squeeze page for your lead magnet. No matter the page's content, however, it needs to match the content of the ad and the visitor's expectations. Anything else is at best confusing and at worst misleading, and it won't do you any favors for growing your conversions.

Speaking of landing pages, keep your engagement offer in mind as you design them. As we mentioned earlier, an engagement offer is the special offer you give to visitors in exchange for an email address. Sometimes, it makes sense for your ad to lead to a squeeze page that directly describes this offer and encourages visitors to sign up. Other times, if you're driving visitors toward a specific product or category page, it makes more sense to display your engagement offer on the page's sidebar. Something as simple as "Sign up today for more great offers" can entice someone to click and lead them to ultimately handing over an email address.

Social Media Ads: Engaging Leads

An alternative is paid social ads – basically getting your product in front of prospects who aren't searching for you but might like what you have to offer. With paid social ads (usually ads on Facebook or Instagram), you're looking to increase your brand awareness to a targeted audience.

Social media has exploded in recent years, becoming one of the most effective forms of online advertising. Whether you run a brick-and-mortar retail store, e-commerce site, affiliate website, or if you are just a local service provider, you can benefit from the use of social media. Maintaining an active presence on networks like Facebook and Twitter will boost your brand recognition while driving more customers to your business.

However, the effectiveness of a social media campaign relies largely on the number of shares your content receives.

1. Make It Emotional

If you scan through the Facebook pages of some of the country's leading brands, you will notice a pattern: the content they choose to post is highly emotional and engaging. Social media users are more likely to share content if it triggers an emotional response. Whether it's an image, video, text, or just a link, focus your social media efforts on emotional, engaging content and you'll find that shares come more naturally.

2. Simple Designs

One of the most common social media mistakes business owners make is posting complex images. Why is this a problem? Even if it successfully conveys your message, many users may overlook it simply because there's too much going on. Numerous studies have shown that simple images and designs are more visually appealing than complex ones. Rather than writing text over an image, for instance, try placing the text on a single-color background (of contrasting color). This practice allows the text to "pop," making it more attractive and easier on the eyes.

3. Make It Relevant

When posting images to social media, make sure they are relevant to your brand's image and what it stands for. This tip may sound like common sense, but you would be surprised to see some of the off-the-wall images and content published by some brands. If you run a dog training service, for instance, the bulk of your social media content should be focused on dogs. Just because you come across a cute picture of a cat doesn't necessarily mean that it's right for your Facebook page. Keep your posts relevant and meaningful to boost your social shares.

4. Color Matters

You might be surprised to learn that the colors of your social media content will affect the number of shares it receives. According to a study conducted by Georgia Tech, content containing red, purple and pink yield the most shares, whereas green, black, blue and yellow get the least number of shares. Why do social media users prefer to share red, purple and pink? According to the study's researchers, it's because these colors trigger visceral emotions in the observer, such as excitement, anxiety, and even fear.

5. Analyze

Above all else, keep an eye on your social media accounts to see which types of content users are sharing and which ones they aren't. Using this information, you can optimize your social media strategy to encourage likes, shares, comments, and other forms of engagement.

To maximize effectiveness, you can combine paid search ads with paid social ads. A prospect searches for a product like yours and is interested enough to click through to your site from a paid search ad but doesn't immediately make a purchase. Later, when the prospect is on Facebook or Instagram, ads pops up reminding them of their interest in your product and keeping your product top-of-mind.

Display Ads on Websites

The third form of online advertising is ads you pay to display on other websites. Paid display ads like the banners on the tops or sides of websites can also be a source of quick leads. Don't just do those without investing in paid search or paid social though, as they're an accessory to those methods, not a good stand-alone. This is because they're a more passive method of advertising compared to search and social methods, which is not sufficient on its own for a digital marketing strategy.

Where display ads really will help your business is through remarketing - where you follow your past site visitors around to other sites through the use of cookies and display your ads for them there. We've all browsed a new pair of shoes on Amazon and seen ads for those exact shoes on another site we visited later that day - that's remarketing. It's so effective because it keeps your potential customer reminded of the product you already know they're interested in and offers them an easy way to go back to it. Google has its own Display Ad offering that's easy to set up and use.

Nurturing Your Leads into Sales

Your ads are up and running, your leads list is organized and segmented, and you're ready to sell.

But it's not quite that quick – you need to nurture your potential customers until a sale is made. This is because prospects don't always buy the first time or even the fourth time. They see you – they get distracted by their dog pawing at the door, ponder checking somewhere else, or think "maybe at my next paycheck" and forget to return. So nurturing is key to keeping your brand as the authority in your space in the eyes of those prospects consistently over time.

How Can You Do This?

Your sustained lead strategy plays a big part in this process. However, it is that you're creating your content (blog, social media, or both) – it all keeps your prospects engaged and interested if you're doing it right.

And here's where the next phase comes in. How are those prospects getting this content?

You need to make sure you have a way of reminding them of you regularly. You might be targeting across the whole country for your technology consulting firm. Or, you might be doing some local digital marketing for your sushi restaurant. However, you are nurturing prospects, continued brand awareness keeps them thinking of you.

The Importance of Email

Email marketing is a critical channel to nurture your prospects. I often advise my clients to start with a series of 5-7 emails when a prospect first shows interest. These aren't just sales emails – they re-introduce your company, and then go on to speak to certain segments of your audience with specific emails that point to blog posts.

For example, if you're a medical specialist group, you might have one email that talks about holistic wellness, then one about aesthetic procedures, and finally one about chronic disease treatment. Then as these go out, you can see which customers click onto those related blog posts, and you get a stronger idea of their interests. This is a great start – you can contact them now with information and products you know they're intrigued by based on their past behavior.

But you can't stop there.

All that great SEO-friendly content you're putting out regularly on your blog? Make sure it doesn't get lost in the noisy world of the web. Send a regular digest email to your online list with your latest 3-5 blog posts – you can send this weekly, monthly, or whatever works with your posting schedule. Your email list might not open every single digest, but they'll see you in their inbox and remember you and your products and services. This is like a billboard on the highway you pass every day on your commute to work – there in the background even when you're just driving along thinking about what to have for dinner. But it keeps your brand awareness subtly top of mind for your prospective customers.

Share Away on Social

You also need to be sure to push those blog posts or articles to the relevant social media channels. This is another non-invasive way you stay connected with your prospects, nurturing that relationship until they're ready to become a customer.

One big success story from a client of mine is Michelle Prince, a motivational speaker and best-selling author. She sells out every Book Bound workshop she holds at ever-increasing numbers. And she does it by diligently collecting email addresses and continuing to drive thoughtful email campaigns regularly. Her clients and prospects feel they get to know her and what she has to offer. By the time she runs a workshop, they're ready to join and are already convinced of the value she's offering.

Do all of this right and you'll find continuous conversions to inquiries and then to those all-important sales.

Keep Up the Momentum

Once your lead generation tactics above are in place, make sure you don't just set it and forget it. The digital marketing world changes quickly. I'd recommend having a review process in place for your digital marketing plan at least once a quarter - look at what's still working and what's stopped working, what's costing you a lot for too little return, and researching if there are any new platforms you should be trying.

Part of this review session should be taking a close look at your leads as well - are there any gaps you're seeing in the sales funnel? Any areas where you need to see growth but aren't? Maybe your IQLs are suffering because your lead magnets aren't working as well as they used to - this is important data.

In the next chapter, we'll talk in much more depth about how to measure the effectiveness of your advertising and lead generation.

Exercise 6:

Take stock of your current advertising strategy, if you have one - are you spread too thin, focused too narrowly, or maybe in the perfect middle? You don't want all your lead eggs in one basket - you need a mix to be sure you can reach your leads effectively wherever they are on the internet.

_____

_____

_____

_____

_____

_____

_____

_____

_____

_____

Chapter 7

LEADS: HOW TO MEASURE SUCCESS

Leads

Social, Search, Display

We've covered how important leads are to generating real, measurable results for your business, and how to generate them from a wide variety of digital marketing strategies. But once those strategies are in place, how can you tell if they're working? Just measuring overall business results isn't enough - an uptick in sales could be due to many factors. By getting thoughtful about how you analyze the rich data that your digital marketing efforts will provide, you can discover exactly what is working best for your business, and what needs improvement.

When calculating the effectiveness of your lead generation efforts, there are a few broad criteria that will help you measure the results of your efforts.

First, how many leads of any kind are you getting from each channel? Are most of them coming from your email marketing campaigns, your social media pages, your paid quick leads, or your sustained leads based on SEO and content? Then, how many of those initial leads convert through the lead process? As a reminder from Chapter 5, here are the types of leads:

Information Qualified Leads (IQL) are when a lead first connects with your business. They have given their contact info in exchange for some piece of valuable content, such as an eBook or free download. IQLs usually don't know a lot about your business or how you can help them.

Marketing Qualified Leads (MQL) has interest and has moved passed the stage of IQL. They understand what you're offering and are considering your solution, shown by downloading or interacting with your content.

Sales Qualified Leads (SQL) is ready to close the sale. They've shown interest in your business, have downloaded your content, have requested a consultation or something similar. They're ready to make a decision.

Looking at where you're struggling to convert leads can be illuminating. For example, if you're getting a lot of IQLs, that's a good sign that the content you're offering is attractive to your potential customers. They're interested in what you have to say.

That's the first step to a sale. But if you're having trouble getting those IQLs into SQLs, there is a gap in what your free content is offering and what value your leads feel they'll get from becoming a paying customer.

These gaps are a chance to look more deeply into your lead management process as a whole - does your content present a compelling argument for why your product or service is necessary for your leads? Do you have a thoughtful process in place for moving leads along in their journey to a sale? Analyzing the data you have should illustrate where you need improvement. This is critical to reducing waste in your marketing budget. After all, if you're spending thousands of dollars on content creation every month, but your content isn't getting your leads to become customers, you need to change your course to a more effective conversion method.

Looking at your leads just by their volume is a helpful first step. But to really get you to the next level in conquering your leads, we need to talk about how to get the highest-value leads for your business.

The best way to do this is to calculate the Lifetime Value of a customer, client, or patient. Many times, business owners look at a single transaction when calculating the success (or failure) of a campaign. The lifetime value of a patient, client, or customer is what needs to be used. This means how much money they'll spend with your company over the course of their lifetime.

For example, if a specialty medical practice offers therapies that lead to other therapies, I take into account the probability that a new patient will continue with additional therapies. If service 1 costs $300 and service 2 costs $500 and service 3 costs $400 and the probability of service 2 is 50% and the probability of service 3 is 50%, then the LTV is $300 + ($500 * 50%) + (50%*($400 * 50%)) = $650. From there, take into account the average number of years a patient stays with a practice and the average annual spend and you a good idea of the true LTV.

Why is this calculation so critical? Because it helps you think about your customer growth over the long term, to set you up for future success. If you have a paid search campaign, maybe you are spending $5 to acquire a customer through Google Ads on average. If your product costs $20, that's a decent profit margin if you just look at the immediate cost. But if all the customers you're getting through search ads buy your cheapest product, and they only buy it once, their lifetime value is low. Maybe you're spending $15 to gain sustained leads through your content, but those leads purchase more expensive products and they come back to your business over and over again, twice a year for 10 years. That lifetime value really begins to add up, and that increased up-front cost of the content creation looks much more reasonable.

This is why gathering and properly analyzing data is so critical to getting measurable results from your marketing spend - it lets you know what's working, what's worth spending, and what's just a budget drain.

Metrics to Measure Your Ad Effectiveness

We've talked a lot about how to measure the effectiveness of your lead strategy. And that's critical, obviously, to gauging the success of your lead generation efforts. Once you've identified where you're losing leads, what do you do? Taking a look at each individual component of your marketing strategy and the data within can provide answers. Here are the four most important metrics to measure when you run a paid ad campaign, and what they mean.

Total Reach

This answers the question, "How many people have seen my ad campaign?" Usually, the higher your budget, the greater your total reach. How does that happen, and how can you maximize your reach if your budget is limited? This metric can be helpful if you're struggling to get IQLs from your paid search or paid social campaigns. If no one is seeing your ads, they can't be enticed by them.

With a bigger budget, your ad can run longer, outbid competitors, and reach more people, but to make sure those clicks convert to sales or appointments, you have to create ads that target the right clients. Use keywords specific to your niche and location. Vague ads will hurt your pocket. Total reach will only be a cause for celebration if it translates to click-through rates (CTR).

Click-Through Rates (CTR)

This answers the question, "How many people clicked on my ad when they saw it?" You know your ad is effective if your click-through rates are high. If 10 people saw your ad and all 10 clicked on it, your rate is 100%, whereas if only five clicked on it, then your rate is 50%.

Again, having a 100% click-through rate may be good but still not a cause to rejoice. Until it converts into a new business, it simply means your ad was attractive enough to hook someone to click on the link.

But if your click-through rate is low, then you need to improve your ad. You may be using the wrong keywords or may not be enticing enough to capture your reader's attention. It can mean you're not speaking to the problems of your target audience or failing to provide information they find valuable.

Cost Per Lead

This answers the question, "How much did I spend for each person who became a lead?" Google would describe this as your total number of conversions - the amount of people who found information about your product or service and are now potential customers.

Usually, you set the maximum price you're willing to pay for each click on your ad. If you set $0.10 as your cost per click and five people clicked on the ad, then you pay $0.50 for those clicks.

With Google Ads, you may even pay less because of bid adjustments. You can also create an ad group for your ads that have a similar target audience. Each group will have keywords that you can set a bid price for.

If out of the five people, only two made an appointment, then your cost per lead is $0.25. The more conversions, the cheaper the cost of your ad campaign.

Cost Per Sale

This answers the question, "How much did I spend for each person who bought a product, became a client, or joined my practice as a patient?" It's almost the same as the cost per lead, but you track sales instead of leads.

Analyze Your Email Marketing Data

Just like your paid ads, it's critical to measure how effective your email campaigns are. While the cost for email campaigns are generally lower than for ads, they can be one of the most effective ways to drive leads to become sales. But this only applies if your emails are working for your business. What metrics do you use to measure the effectiveness of your email marketing campaign? Many marketers are left in the dark about their email marketing performance. You shouldn't be.

What metrics do savvy marketers use?

Click-through Rates

About 91% of marketers measure the effectiveness of their email marketing campaign using click-through rates. You can do the same. Typically, click-through rates monitor the number of people who click on your emails, as I discussed above.

You can also embed links in your emails that will invite your readers to visit your website for more information. This is called a call-to-action button. You'll find out how many of your readers, who opened the email, clicked on the link within the email. This is an easy way to gauge general interest - if no one you send an email to is clicking on your CTAs, they're not strong enough and some testing and re-writing is needed to make them more effective.

Open Rates

Another way to analyze the success of your email marketing campaign is the open rate. About 80% of marketers use this metric. Most emails are left unopened when they fail to hook your readers with your subject lines.

Here's a useful rule of thumb. Your subject line should hint at a solution to your reader's problem, and that solution is something better than what they have tried before. This is basically the anatomy of a great subject line.

The promise that you make will cause the reader to click and read. A word of caution: keep your promise and honestly deliver so you'll gain their trust and not ignore your email the second time around.

Conversion Rate

You should set up tracking URLs to see how many of your readers clicked on your link and then acted on a call-to-action button. This means you've converted a reader or prospect to a client or customer.

For instance, a company that sells luggage might send out an email about packing efficiently for long trips. At the end, they may add a button that leads the reader to their website to learn more about the topic. And in that page, they may have a call-to-action button to buy a suitcase or a travel accessory. Tracking this conversion and others like it will tell you how well your emails are doing at making your prospects on your email list into paying customers. Call tracking can be a very effective method of calculating how much interest your emails are getting, which I'll talk about in the next section.

Bounce Rate

There are two types of bounce rates:

Hard bounces are those that come from invalid email addresses, which will result in permanent errors. Once you receive this kind of error, contact the recipient for an updated email address. There could just have been a misspelled letter.

Soft bounces, on the other hand, are temporary but will give you clues about your recipients' behavior. For instance, a full inbox will give a soft bounce. This can either mean a stagnant email address that the person uses for consumer-related emails or the owner of the email address rarely opens and reads her emails.

Your email may have also been marked as spam. Is this a sign that you're sending more emails than valued or appreciated by your prospects? You can improve your bounce rates by filtering subscriber preferences when it comes to what kind of emails they appreciate or want to read in their inboxes.

Delivery Rate

In place of the bounce rate, you can monitor the delivery rate instead. If your email didn't bounce, it simply means it got delivered to the right recipient. Typically, you'd want a 90% delivery rate. Otherwise, you need some serious cleaning of your email list.

But take note that delivery rate doesn't necessarily mean your recipient opened your email. It simply means it got to their inbox. It can be left unopened and ignored or deleted with nary a glance.

List Growth Rate

Make sure your list is growing every year. This means you are acquiring new contacts in your mailing list more than you are deleting stagnant email addresses. There are several ways to grow your email list. First, ensure your website has multiple places where a person who finds your content interesting can sign up easily to stay in touch. Some good places could be on your landing page, on your footer, and interspersed into blogs posts where relevant. Second, develop enticing lead magnets - free content you offer in exchange for a prospect's email address. The lead magnet should be something that speaks to your audience's needs in order to be effective.

Why You Need Call Tracking

Let's get offline for a second. Tracking the ways leads find you through the internet and make an online purchase is great. With the amount of time we all spend online, it's critical. But one key driver of sales can slip through the analytics cracks - phone calls. After all, if you get a call from an interested potential customer, you might have no idea where they found your information. A Google review page? Your Instagram account? An email you sent?

If you're in a business where your customers will pick up the phone and call you, you can miss out on really useful data if you don't set up call tracking. So, what is it, exactly?

Let's use an example of a landscaping company. If a customer performs a Google search for "landscaping companies near me" and up comes that company's Google ad, it might have a phone number in it. If the customer just types in that phone number without clicking through the ad, then the landscaper has no idea that this ad just earned them a lead. They might decide their Google Ads campaign isn't working as well as they hoped, and cancel it based on inaccurate information.

This is where call tracking comes in. Essentially, you create and then track different phone numbers for each campaign instead of using the same phone number in all your ads. Then, the call tracking software will calculate how many calls each campaign is generating and give you a fuller picture of how well your campaigns are performing. This tracking has a lot of benefits for your digital marketing campaigns. It can tell you which keywords are performing best for your pay-per-click ads, which display ads are converting well into leads, and what organic search traffic is leading to prospective customer calls.

Call tracking is critical to getting a full picture of your marketing results. Taking the landscaping company we talked about above, they might have some interesting big-picture findings once they implement call tracking. Maybe those Google Ads are proving much more successful than they'd thought at first, leading to a high volume of calls that convert to sales. But if they'd been spending a much higher portion of their budget on Instagram ads, thinking those were converting well, that picture changes with the call tracking if suddenly the Instagram ads are looking pricier in cost-per-sale metrics.

Call tracking also allows you to listen in on calls to your business, which can identify other ways you're losing leads. Perhaps that landscaping company finds their receptionist can be curt or unhelpful with potential clients, or their salespeople need more training in the services on offer.

Clearly, call tracking can offer a wealth of information that will help you discover possible avenues where you're getting (or losing) more leads than expected. It's a useful way to determine the effectiveness of your overall marketing, especially if you're in an industry where you get a lot of phone inquiries. It can seem old-school or counterintuitive to focus on phone metrics when you're measuring digital marketing, but it will give you a fuller picture of your marketing ROI and help you cut out waste and invest in what's working well for you.

Measuring How Your Content Converts

We've talked in several previous chapters about how important a strong content creation strategy is when building your digital marketing. But how can you tell if it's working to gain you leads and sales? After all, creating thoughtful, insightful, helpful content on a consistent basis can be costly in time, money, or both.

So, what are the metrics you need to measure to see if your investment in content is paying off in leads and sales? Many of the metrics are similar to the email and ad campaign measurements above. If you have calls to action to promote your services in most of your blog posts (and you should!), check your Google Analytics to see if your readers are clicking on those links, or just reading and leaving without taking an action. Are your prospects downloading your free eBooks and white papers but then not taking any further action? This could be because the information you offer there is so comprehensive they end up not needing your services, or because it's too vague to give them a true idea of your value as an expert.

Much measuring of content conversion goes along with email metrics as well - you're sending those great blog posts out as digest emails, right? (If not, that's the first place you need to start to increase your conversion rates).

If you're really stuck on why your content isn't converting as well as you'd hope, it can be helpful to do some opposition research. Find one of your competitors in your industry and take a peek at their blog. How different does it look from yours? Is there something they're doing differently that you could experiment with? Testing out stronger headlines or bolder CTAs could be worthwhile to get your conversion rate higher.

Takeaways

Ultimately, each part of your digital marketing strategy works together to find you leads and convert them into sales. Nothing operates in isolation - your emails link to your blog posts, and your ads take leads to your website or to your phone number. You can't afford to neglect one or most portions. Getting a thorough understanding of the metrics of each area is important - don't assume one piece is working if you haven't looked at the numbers. Using the data to assess where your most efficient lead generation and conversion is occurring is key to maximizing your ROI. Fortunately, access to that data has never been easier than it is with digital marketing. So, don't let that data go to waste.

Exercise 7:

Pick one of the metrics areas I discussed above - ads, email, calls, or content - where your business could use the most help. Do a deep dive into how those lead sources are converting to sales - do the math to get a hard number on that. Then, brainstorm one change you could try fairly easily to get that conversion number increasing. It could be adding clearer CTAs in your emails, writing stronger headlines for your blog articles, writing a new search ad, or testing out one call tracking software.

_____

_____

_____

_____

_____

_____

_____

_____

_____

_____

.

Chapter 8

Nurture: What Is It?

Blog, Digest,
eMail Campaigns,
Social Posts

What Is Nurture Marketing?

So now you've reached the exciting part – the sales portion!

Your online presence is up and running and beautifully thought through, your content strategy is in place, and you're ready to sell.

But it's not quite that quick – you need to nurture your potential customers until a sale is made. This is because prospects don't always buy the first time or even the fourth time. They see you – they get distracted by their dog pawing at the door, ponder checking somewhere else, or think "maybe at my next paycheck" and forget to return. Nurturing is key to keeping your brand as the authority in your space in the eyes of those prospects consistently over time. Think of it as a series of gentle nudges that remind leads who have shown interest in your product that they can benefit from what you offer.

In a nutshell, nurture marketing is the process of value creation through sharing worthwhile, useful content with prospects based on their interests and behaviors. Sounds like a mouthful, right?

In fact, it's quite simple when you break it down. Nurture marketing campaigns effectively create and maintain a conversation by consistently adapting to the prospect's replies (or lack thereof).

In our opinion, nurture marketing is the heart and soul of a content marketing strategy. It's more than just putting out content, sending an email, posting to social media, or creating a website.

It's an avenue for building strong, meaningful customer relationships that drive revenue and client satisfaction. Hopefully, you're already doing this in other ways. But nurture marketing takes things to the next level, by expanding your reach and solidifying your presence in your particular marketplace.

So, at the moment a prospect is ready to buy, they think of you first.

What Does Nurture Marketing Look Like?

A common example of nurture marketing is through an email campaign.

For example, when someone subscribes to your email newsletter, they'll immediately be sent a "welcome" email to confirm their subscription and perhaps share a bit about what they can expect in forthcoming messages, links to your social pages, etc.

In a series of subsequent messages, the prospect will be sent valuable content, such as blog posts, videos, webinars, etc. What begins as a "soft sell" begins to close the gap between "maybe" to "I'm ready to buy."

Managing leads used to be the responsibility of the sales team — endless cold calls, unanswered emails, offering products prospects may or may not be interested in…

Nurture marketing is a bit subtler, yet magnificently more effective. Instead of guessing at what your prospect wants, nurture marketing pays attention to the behaviors of your prospects to offer targeted offers, info, and services they actually want.

For example, say you send your list a link to download a free chapter of your eBook. To everyone who downloaded the chapter, you send a thank you message with an additional link to a related webinar.

Anyone that clicks to view the webinar will be contacted by your sales team. The prospect has demonstrated considerable interest, and the salesperson is much more likely to convert them.

How Does It Work?

To accomplish this, you offer them free value through various forms of content (blogs, social media, eBooks, webinars, free downloads, emails, etc.) When you offer something of extreme value to a prospect, without asking for anything in return, you naturally create a basis of trust.

Once you've gained the trust of a prospect, it's time to listen. By using data and analytics to see how they respond and interact with the content you share, you're able to give them even more of what they love.

For example, say I create a series of three emails, all including links to different blog posts, targeting different topics. If a prospect opens email #2, discussing the best times to post on social media, I can be pretty sure they're interested in learning more about social media. Thus, I can send them additional content tailored to their interests.

Nurture marketing, although heavily reliant on automation, is an extremely personal form of marketing. It takes into consideration the actions and engagement of a prospect or client, in order to serve them even better.

Who Should Use Nurture Marketing?

To help you understand if your organization should use nurture marketing, consider the following:

1. Where do you get your leads?

   By far, the best way to get leads is through referrals. Nurture marketing generates warm leads by way of building trust and rapport before you even hint at a sale.

2. What is your follow-up mechanism?

   Once you have a lead, how do you keep in touch with them? Oftentimes, you give them a call, right? But what happens when they don't pick up or you're sent to voicemail? Do you keep calling? Nurture marketing is a more time-efficient way to interact with a prospect every couple of days or weeks via email, social media and so on, without anyone falling through the cracks.

3. What happens to those who don't close?

   Maybe your prospect isn't ready to buy now. But who's to say in 2, 3, 4 months, things won't be different? How do you stay in touch? Nurture marketing makes sure you show up, so when they're ready to buy, you're there.

Nurturing Efficiency

Nurture marketing has many benefits for turning new leads into sales. But it also has great benefits for getting customers who have made a purchase or two to return again and again. That repeat business saves you the marketing dollars that would go to acquire a new customer and builds your business a strong foundation for the future.

Nurture marketing also has the advantage of being relatively inexpensive once it's set up, compared to the cost of your other marketing elements. It requires some thoughtful automation, especially via email, but that's hopefully a system you already have set up for your email digests we talked about earlier. Referrals from satisfied customers cost you nothing but pay huge dividends in sales. Essentially, the goal of nurture marketing is to make all your avenues for brand awareness lead to a sale - the ultimate way to make sure your marketing dollars are spent effectively. It will save your sales and marketing staff time as well. By targeting your leads with a low-touch method like personalized emails, they know your value by the time they talk to a salesperson.

Another benefit of nurture marketing is how it makes your leads and customers feel - like your company is a brand they can trust, a name that's an authority in the field, and a brand that looks out for them. You move beyond just being another company trying to sell them something. Since you're being targeted and thoughtful and generous with information in your emails (all that free content with no hard sell!), you are building trust. And you can't buy that with the biggest marketing budget. This kind of effort is what sets your business up to succeed in the long term, not just making sales today. That's why I believe in it, and why you need to try it.

Exercise 8:

Assess if you have any nurture marketing elements in place already. Maybe you have an automated email sequence set up for leads, or a way to segment your leads by interest. Maybe you have a whole sophisticated nurture marketing system in place already, or maybe you have nothing at all. But in either case, take a close look at what already exists in your business and write it down for the next chapter, where we'll take a look at how to build a nurture marketing structure.

_____

_____

_____

_____

_____

_____

_____

_____

_____

Chapter 9

NURTURE: HOW TO DO IT

Nurture

Blog, Digest,
eMail Campaigns,
Social Posts

How do you make nurture marketing work for your business? It can be a big shift to think of nurturing as a marketing strategy that's essential for your business, not just a "nice to have". But as we saw in the last chapter, nurturing your prospects until they're ready to make a purchase is key. It ensures your marketing dollars you've spent on those paid campaigns, thoughtful content, and beautiful website are put to their most effective use. Because it's how you get a lead into a sale, and a sale into a repeat customer.

How can you do this?

Your sustained lead strategy plays a big part in this process. However it is that you're creating your content (blog, social media, or both) – it all keeps your prospects engaged and interested if you're doing it right.

And here's where the next phase comes in. How are those prospects getting this content?

You need to make sure you have a way of reminding them of you regularly. You might be targeting across the whole country for your technology consulting firm. Or, you might be doing some local digital marketing for your sushi restaurant. However you are nurturing prospects, continued brand awareness keeps them thinking of you.

The Importance of Email

Email marketing is a critical channel to nurture your prospects. I often advise our clients to start with a series of 5-7 emails when a prospect first shows interest. There are a variety of email automation programs out there that can help with this portion. MailChimp or Keap are good for solo entrepreneurs, InfusionSoft and Hubspot are good for small businesses, and Pardot or Marketo are great for bigger companies.

Why is setting up strong email marketing critical to effective marketing?

Instant Marketing

While traditional forms of advertising — radio commercials, television commercials, billboards, etc. — often take days, if not weeks, to set up and run, email marketing is virtually instant. In just seconds after you click the "send" button, your email will be sent to each and every contact on your list. This means you can focus more time on building and expanding your business and less time on micromanaging advertising campaigns.

Valuable Analytics

Assuming you have the proper analytics software in place, email marketing will generate tons of valuable data, such as open rate, click-through rate (CTR), conversion rate, and ROI. Using this data, you can tweak and optimize your email campaigns for better performance. So even if you start off with poor results, the massive amount of analytical data will allow you to turn your campaigns into profitable, sustainable marketing platforms.

Generate Multiple Sales from the Same Customer

Email is unique in the sense that it allows businesses to market their products and services to the same customer multiple times. Once you have a potential customer's email address, you can continue sending him or her promotional emails — assuming they don't opt out. You may generate a single sale from the initial email, but the follow-up emails may generate additional sales.

Cheaper than Traditional Media

According to Experian, one of the three major credit bureaus, email marketing is 20 times more cost effective than traditional media. This statistic alone should be reason enough for small businesses and entrepreneurs to use email marketing.

Eco-Friendly Alternative to 'Snail Mail'

I can't talk about the benefits of email marketing without mentioning its eco-friendly properties. Sending advertisements the old-fashioned way via snail mail is downright expensive and wasteful. Each advertisement requires ink and paper, as well as the resources needed to manufacture and ship the ink and paper. Email, on the other hand, is completely digital, making it a smart choice for the environment.

Powerful Segmentation

This initial series of 5-7 emails aren't just sales emails – they re-introduce your company, and then go on to speak to certain segments of your audience with specific emails that point to blog posts.

For example, if you're a medical specialist group, you might have one email that talks about holistic wellness, then one about aesthetic procedures, and finally one about chronic disease treatment. Then as these go out, you can see which customers click onto those related blog posts, and you get a stronger idea of their interests. This is a great start – you can contact them now with information and products you know they're intrigued by based on their past behavior.

But you can't stop there.

All that great SEO-friendly content you're putting out regularly on your blog? Make sure it doesn't get lost in the noisy world of the web. Send a regular digest email to your online list with your latest 3-5 blog posts – you can send this weekly, monthly, or whatever works with your posting schedule. Your email list might not open every single digest, but they'll see you in their inbox and remember you and your products and services. This is like a billboard on the highway you pass every day on your commute to work – there in the background even when you're just driving along thinking about what to have for dinner. But it keeps your brand awareness subtly top of mind for your prospective customers.

Share Away on Social

You also need to be sure to push those blog posts or articles to the relevant social media channels. This is another non-invasive way you stay connected with your prospects, nurturing that relationship until they're ready to become a customer.

One big success story from my clients is Michelle Prince, a motivational speaker and best-selling author. She sells out every Book Bound workshop she holds at ever-increasing numbers. And she does it by diligently collecting email addresses and continuing to drive thoughtful email campaigns regularly. Her clients and prospects feel they get to know her and what she has to offer. By the time she runs a workshop, they're ready to join and are already convinced of the value she's offering.

Do all of this right and you'll find continuous conversions to inquiries and then to those all-important sales.

Engaging A Targeted Sales Funnel

A sales funnel is a highly effective way to nurture prospects through the conversion process, encouraging them to buy your products or services.

Instead of blasting your ads to a large audience and not following up with those users, you can customize your advertising/marketing experience to yield a stronger response and more sales.

Why do you need a sales funnel? Because sales aren't a one-step process - you don't just tell someone about your product once and get an immediate sale. Your prospects and leads need time to decide and get additional information about your offers. They need to develop trust in you and what you're offering. That's why you need a sales funnel - one with the steps to get you to the sale.

The top of the sales funnel begins with the awareness stage - where your prospects begin to learn who you are and what you offer. This stage is where your marketing is most important. It speaks to your broad target audience and tells them your story. Next, the middle of the funnel is the nurture stage. This is where your marketing department or process makes the case to a narrower pool of leads for your product or service. And the bottom of the funnel? That's where your leads make a decision and take an action - make a purchase or become a client.

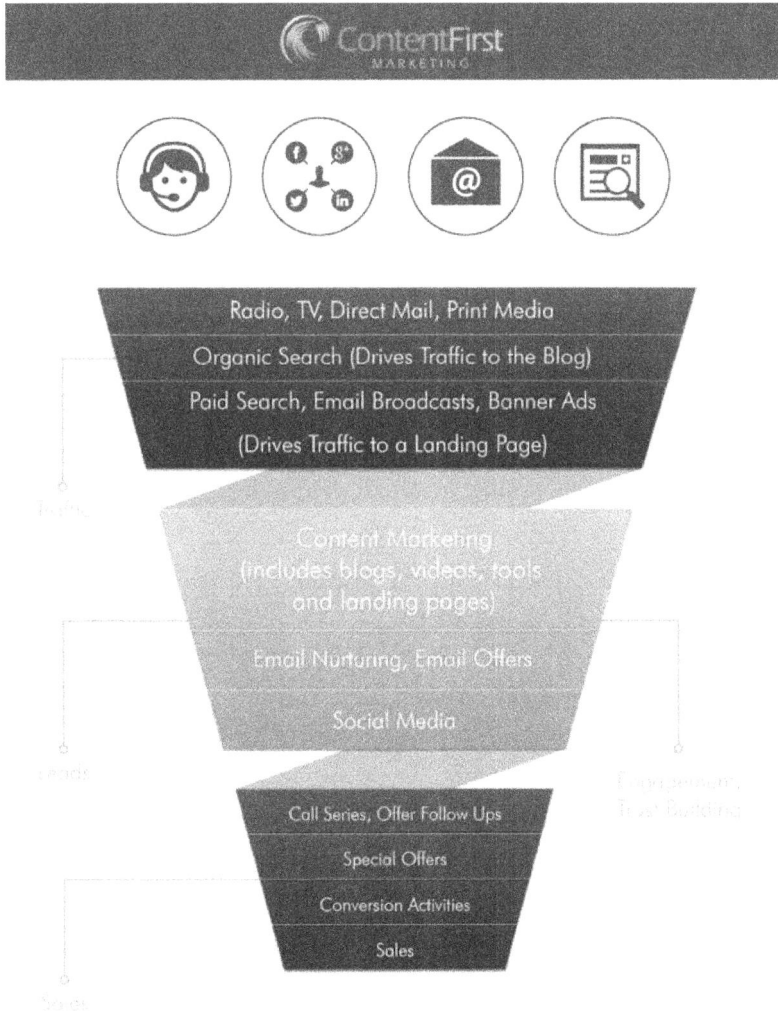

How to optimize your online sales funnel?

1. Start at the Top

One of the biggest mistakes that small business owners and digital marketers make with their online sales funnel is starting at a narrow section of the funnel. Start at the top of the sales funnel first, nurturing these prospects, so they are more likely to buy your products or services.

2. Customize Each Stage of the Sales Funnel

Each stage of your sales funnel should be customized. After all, the entire purpose of a sales funnel is to appeal to a different demographic, nurturing those users through the sales process.

Take a few moments to create a rough draft of your sales funnel, defining each section with a specific focus. You can always go back and restructure your sales funnel, but it's a good idea to have a rough draft on hand for a source of reference.

3. Personalize Emails

There are dozens of ways to attract customers or clients to your sales funnel, but one of the most effective is email. With email, you can personalize your marketing messages and promotional material according to the recipient's demographic.

Here are some tips to improve the effectiveness of your marketing emails and attract more prospects to your sales funnel:

– Set up an email newsletter on your blog or website.

NURTURE: HOW TO DO IT

- Send prospects a combination of both informative, non-commercial emails AND promotional emails.

- Use a recognizable "from" name.

- Use a mobile-friendly email template, preferably designed with a responsive theme.

- Clean up your email list on a regular basis, removing duplicate and inactive emails.

- Keep your subject lines under 60 characters for maximum visibility.

- Customize your preview line - what customers will see along with the subject line when the unopened email is in their inbox. Preview text should support the subject line to encourage opening the email.

- Split test different timings and frequencies for your emails.

One promising alternative to email is SMS or text messages. These are more immediate and urgent - great for getting timely information to your prospects. These need to be much shorter than emails but can be effective for promotions. Just be sure to check spam laws in your state to ensure you're in compliance.

4. Create a Strong Content Strategy

You can't expect to have a successful sales funnel without a strong content marketing strategy. Content is a fundamental component of any online sales funnel process, as it allows the business owner to engage with his or her prospects and keep them interested in their respective product or service.

5. Identify the Bottom of Your Sales Funnel

Of course, the bottom of your sales funnel is arguably the most important section. This is where prospects take action - making a decision about whether to purchase your product or service. But you'll need to determine what this action is. For an e-commerce site, the bottom of the sales funnel may consist of a sale. For a medical practice, it could be a patient making their first appointment. The last stage is a sale "won", or a "lost/deferred".

6. Get Back Lost Prospects

Just because a prospect backs out of your sales funnel doesn't mean that he or she is a lost sale. There are ways to recapture these prospects, encouraging them to come back to your sales funnel. Assuming you have the prospect's email address, for instance, you can send a personalized email, including a special "come back to us" promotional offer.

7. Keep Optimizing!

Even if your sales funnel is currently attracting new customers or clients and generating sales, you should continue optimizing it for a higher conversion rate and better return on investment (ROI), because there's ALWAYS room for improvement. Continue analyzing your sales funnel's metrics and split-testing different promotional material to see what works and what doesn't.

Leading to Success

Strong nurture marketing campaigns also require some thoughtful sorting of your leads into those categories we discussed earlier. As you're thinking of your strategy to take prospects through the sales funnel, think of what each type of lead is looking for. Information qualified leads (IQLs) have shown a general interest in your content. Marketing qualified leads (MQLs) are more seriously engaging with what you're offering. And sales qualified leads (SQLs) are ready to make a purchase. What steps do you need to take to get each kind of lead to the next level?

An Example of Nurture Marketing (At the Dentist!)

Let me give you an example of the last time I experienced nurture marketing: at my dentist's office. In fact, I noticed it on two separate occasions.

The first time was after a cleaning appointment. Before the day was over, I got a personalized email from my dentist, thanking me for coming in and offering an incentive for reviewing them on Yelp!

By simply recommending my dentist (who I already know and trust), they offered me a FREE $5 Starbucks gift card. How could I pass up a free coffee?

How Did the Dentist Accomplish Nurture Marketing?

My dentist is building a relationship with me by connecting right after my appointment and letting me know I'm a valued patient.

What's more, they're offering me something of value (who doesn't love free coffee?) in exchange for a referral. Through one simple automated email, they're nurturing two relationships: the existing and also the prospective client.

The second instant happened a few days later, and this is an example I love. During my appointment, my dentist recommended a dental surgeon for my wisdom teeth extraction. They gave me a quote for the procedure, as well as the contact information of the surgeon.

Two days later, I received an email: "Have you scheduled your wisdom teeth removal?" Amazing. Within the body was the same info I received at my appointment, including a digital copy of my quote.

How Is This Nurture Marketing?

Just like the first example, they're following up with me and letting me know they care about my treatment. Secondly, they're nurturing their relationship with the dental surgeon by recommending qualified patients to their office. You can bet when that dental surgeon has a patient due for a cleaning, they'll be referring my dentist.

The Bottom Line

Nurture marketing is the business of following up.

Are you following up with your leads?

Could you be following up more?

If you are following up, how effective are your methods?

Nurture marketing ensures that you are at the forefront of consumer minds, so when they're ready to make a purchase, they'll choose you. The time you take to follow up will never be a waste: it is a true investment in your consumer and your business.

There are tons of ways to follow up, but one thing you must always do is offer something of value. In the example of my dentist they offered two things:

1. A free coffee

2. A qualified, trusted source for further treatment

Now that you know what nurture marketing is, where have you experienced it? Check your inbox for clues.

Exercise 9:

Sit down with a pen and paper and draw a rough outline of your sales funnel. With your current leads, who is at the top, middle, and bottom? Once you've determined that, take a look at approximately how many leads you have in each category. Is there one area where the leads are getting held up? This is important information as you move forward with creating your nurture marketing strategy - which can help those stalled leads move into the sales column. What gaps or blocks are you seeing?

_____

_____

_____

_____

_____

_____

_____

_____

_____

_____

Chapter 10

NURTURE: HOW TO MEASURE SUCCESS

Nurture

Blog, Digest,
eMail Campaigns,
Social Posts

You've now seen how nurture marketing can make a huge impact on your business while spending your marketing dollars effectively. Now let's get into measuring your nurture marketing campaigns - are they working for you? Fortunately, with the data available from digital marketing, gauging your success is simple. The goal of nurture marketing is to move your leads along your sales funnel with high engagement and low friction until they're ready to make a decision and take an action. So, how well is your nurture marketing working for your business?

Measuring Lead Conversions

One of the most important ways to measure the success of your marketing efforts is to evaluate the effectiveness of your sales funnel. As we talked about in the last chapter, your sales funnel is the way you convert awareness into sales in a series of steps. The steps will be different for each business. But you can measure the effectiveness of your sales funnel in a few ways.

Monitor Metrics

As with any online marketing and advertising campaign, it's important to monitor key performance indicators (KPIs) throughout your sales funnel.

- How many prospects are abandoning the funnel?

- How many are following through to the next step?

- What is their level of engagement?

- How many prospects are clicking on your call-to-action?

Let's get in-depth about your KPIs.

Conversion Rate From MQL to SQL

Marketing qualified leads (MQLs) are at the top of the sales funnel - they're aware of your brand and product but not ready to buy yet. Sales qualified leads have moved to the next step - they're getting ready to take action. So what is your rate of conversation from MQL to SQL? To calculate this, you simply divide the number of SQLs by the number of MQLs. Be sure to take into account the time frame of your sales cycle - if a sale cycle for your business usually takes six months, don't just take the number of leads in a one-month period. Average conversion rate will vary by industry and product, so do a little research to see where you stack up. This rate will give you a good idea of how well your marketing is converting interest into actionable leads.

Close Rate on SQLs

Your next calculation is gauging how many of your SQLs become sales. Like the previous metric, you calculate your SQL close rate by dividing your number of closes by the number of SQLs. This number gives you a picture of how effectively your sales efforts are resulting in a positive action. Again, this is an area where you need to take into account your typical sales cycle length while calculating, so you can be sure you get an accurate view.

Look at the Big Picture

Take a look at your sales funnel as a whole - accounting for each inner stage. What is the rate of leads who drop out at each stage? This gets into more detail than the MQL>SQL conversion rate. It tells you where leads are dropping out of the funnel. And that tells you where your bottlenecks or pain points are in your sales funnel. For example, maybe you're getting plenty of leads in the top of the funnel with the free information you offer. That tells you positive data - what you're offering in your content has value for your leads. They like it enough to take an action by giving you their email address. But perhaps they drop out once you've made your initial sales contact. This drop-out rate indicates some kind of missed opportunity - following up too aggressively or not following up enough, misdirecting leads into the sales department instead of to a nurture campaign, or more. Research will help you determine what the issue is and allow you to fix it before you lose more leads. Think creatively - the pain point could be something unexpected. I've abandoned shopping websites that aren't optimized for mobile purchases, even if I found their product attractive. Small issues can have big consequences.

How engaged are your leads in your sales funnel? If the funnel is too wide, you might have a lot of leads with low engagement - they don't open most of your emails, read most of your content, or respond to social media posts. This is a problem because it could lead your sales department to waste valuable time on leads who are not likely to convert. If you find you have a lot of leads with low engagement, evaluate your content for clues. Maybe your blog strategy is too vague, your social media persona too bland, or your emails too lacking in CTAs. Whatever is causing your low engagement rate, fixing it will narrow your sales funnel to leads who are the most likely to convert. This will ensure you're not wasting your marketing dollars by casting too wide a net.

Evaluate Your Leads by Source

Another piece of valuable data is where you're getting your highest-conversion leads. Use the data you've collected to separate out your leads by source (this is where your call-tracking software is very useful as well). This information helps determine if you're spending your marketing dollars wisely. If you're pouring most of your marketing budget into pay-per-click ads and getting many leads there, but very few of them convert into sales, you need to reallocate those dollars or reevaluate your strategy. Noting that one source of leads isn't converting well doesn't always mean you should abandon it. If your email campaigns aren't converting, or your content is struggling, look at why they're failing. A new strategy, like stronger headlines or clearer CTAs, could fix the problem.

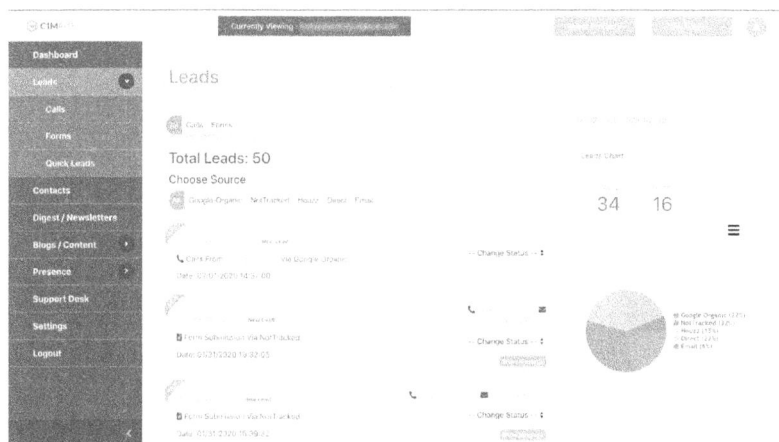

The Importance of Customer Relationship Management

If you've read all the strategies above about how to track and evaluate leads and conversions and feel a little lost, don't panic. This is especially common for new companies or solo entrepreneurs. It can seem like too much data to manage at one time when you're just getting started. But there's a solution.

Customer relationship management (CRM) refers to the strategies and processes businesses use to manage interactions with customers, sales prospects, and suppliers.

CRM focuses on building and maintaining long-lasting relationships with all stakeholders (not to be confused with shareholders). A CRM system is software that allows a business to build and manage relationships more efficiently and effectively, which in turn results in higher sales and revenue.

Before, CRM systems originally were very costly and only used by large organizations. But now many vendors such as Keap are making CRM systems that are affordable and beneficial to small and mid-size businesses. CRM systems allow businesses to store and access all of their data — sales, marketing, and customer service — in one place. However, these are not just databases merely to store data. Different departments use the data differently, so a CRM system enables teams to collaborate and work toward the same goals while still meeting their individual objectives.

CRM systems give businesses the tools to learn about customers' needs and buying habits, create and improve sales and marketing processes, and provide better customer service throughout the entire customer lifecycle.

How Can a CRM Grow My Business and Boost Sales?

1. Better Customer Service and Customer Experience

A CRM system gives you the ability to personalize and customize interactions with customers. By knowing and anticipating individual customer needs, you can quickly and successfully meet or exceed their expectations. Improved customer service builds a stronger, long-lasting relationship.

2. Improved Marketing Strategies

Learn what works for different customer demographics, which enables you to save money while increasing your customer base. Automated processes simplify and improve communication between you, your prospects, and your customers. Customers have more choices about how and when they want to be approached, which instills loyalty.

3. Simplified Sales Processes

Lead generation and tracking is improved, making for a faster sales cycle. Reduce costs by focusing efforts on only your strongest prospects. You also have a clearer idea of the sales pipeline and the effectiveness of sales members or teams.

4. Save Time While Increasing Revenue

With CRM, you will no longer waste time on marketing efforts that aren't working, chase prospects who won't become customers, and muddle your way through inefficient processes. So, you can instead spend your time focusing on other important things (or take a real vacation!). In addition, because your relationship-building will pay off in increased sales, your revenues will grow.

Almost all CRM systems provide some marketing and sales tools. But many don't include additional features that may prove highly beneficial for your business. Be cautious about jumping into the first or least expensive CRM system you find. Do some research first. You'll learn about the variety of features available before you make a decision on which CRM system to use.

Exercise 10:

Take the sales funnel you created in the last exercise. Now, take a hard look at it with the data you have available. Determine one place where your leads are dropping out of the sales funnel in larger numbers than you'd expect. Then, brainstorm what the possible pain points they're encountering could be. Is it a clunky part of your website? An email campaign that keeps getting caught in the spam filter? Blog content that is compelling to read, but lacks an action to take? If the pain point is something easy to fix, make the fix! If it requires more effort or a serious investment of time, make a plan to get it fixed in the near future.

_____

_____

_____

_____

_____

_____

_____

_____

_____

Chapter 11

Reputation Management: The Power of Word-of-Mouth

You now know the value of the three-part marketing cycle - developing an online presence, generating leads, and nurturing those leads into a sale. All three of those steps will make your marketing dollars work for you. But there is another step to ensuring those marketing dollars aren't going to waste - managing your online reputation. Why is this so important?

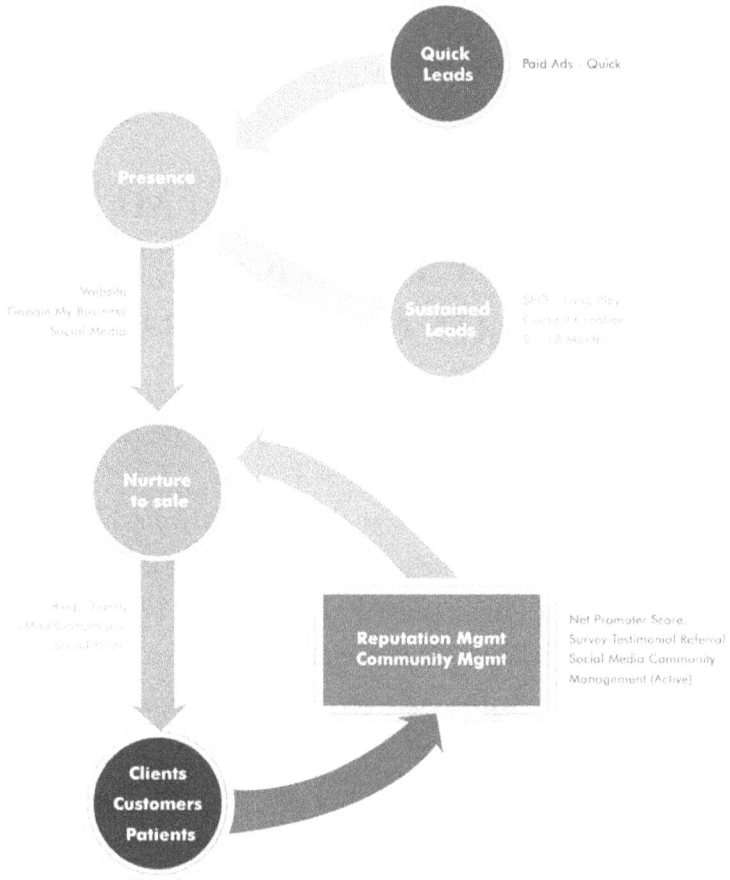

Why Online Reputation Matters

A few years ago, Pepsi put out an unfortunate ad that went viral in a mere matter of minutes — and not for good reasons. What was intended to be a message of peace and understanding backfired completely, and the internet was there for every second of it.

Within a blink of an eye, Pepsi, a world-famous, internationally-loved brand, was condemned by the online community and dubbed "canceled." Every dollar they spent on that worldwide marketing campaign? It wasn't just a waste - it was actively working against them.

Similarly, we all remember what happened to United Airlines after a video leaked of a man being forcibly removed from one of their aircraft. The social media uproar was enough to annihilate the brand entirely. But the follow-up, non-apologetic "apology" letter from the United Airlines CEO only added more fuel to the fire. Months later, United is still fighting to regain their reputation and win back customers.

These complete and total reputation "failures", spurred by online and media attention, are becoming more prevalent. The general population has raised the standard of what they expect from the brands they love and are more willing to call out unfavorable behavior.

Has your brand faced a similar predicament? It may not be on such a massive scale as with Pepsi or United, but even one negative Yelp! review or poorly-worded blog post can cause a tidal wave of negative consequences for your business.

We'll show you how to manage a healthy online reputation while staying true to your brand and the customers you serve.

What is Online Reputation Management (ORM)?

Simply put, it is the way your brand is seen online. That includes everything: from how customers find your business and how they learn about your company, to how you can develop the optimal online presence to connect you with the most customers. ORM also involves how your brand reacts to crisis, deals with difficult situations, and ultimately repairs and strengthens its image.

The biggest misconception about ORM is that it's all about reviews. While it's true that online reviews are a key source of information, consumers are becoming more and more skeptical of their legitimacy. Reviews are just a piece of the puzzle, and if the rest of your online presence falls flat, even the best reviews can't save you.

Why Is It Important?

According to a recent study, there are at least 18 different ways Google can find your brand (not even including social media). Think of the last time you typed something into Google. The search results gave you plenty of options, including images, videos, advertisements, review sites, instant answers, and more.

If a customer wants to learn about your brand, they have plenty of avenues to do so — great news for you, because it means you have just as many opportunities to impress them. Now more than ever, the online experience is customized to the user. Online searches are tailored to the user's language, location, device, previous searches, friends' searches, and so on. Marketers have to get on board with the digital revolution if they want to stay alive.

No One is Searching for Your Brand

Sorry to burst your bubble, but it's true. Unless you're a big-name brand like Walmart, IKEA, Apple, etc., no one is searching for your brand.

Your customers are searching for a solution, service, or information.

Before connecting with a brand, customers will gather the information they need so that when they do reach out, they're ready or almost ready to make a purchase.

ORM factors into the equation by how well you're able to position your brand online. When someone searches for a solution to their problem, does your business come up? Is your online presence making the best use of keywords and phrases that customers are searching on the internet?

Brands can differentiate themselves from competitors by creating a strong online reputation using important keywords that customers frequent in their searches.

Keep in mind, the majority of searches do not include a brand name — they include a solution. For example, "best dishwasher repair", "cheapest landscape maintenance near me", or "good pizza in Dallas."

What Can Cause a Bad Online Reputation?

A misconception about online reputations is that reviews are all that matter, or they are at least the most important factor. In fact, people are pretty suspicious of good reviews.

That's not to say good reviews aren't important and that you shouldn't be asking for them. However, they don't carry as much weight as you'd think. Articles are more meaningful and credible in the eyes of a customer.

One negative article can cancel your whole customer journey. The reason being that unlike reviews, which are all grouped together, an article is a singular entity. It carries a lot more weight.

Because people are so skeptical of good reviews, they turn to other sources of information for more credibility:

- Your Website

- Blogs

- Online Articles

- Press Releases

- Social Proof (how are you involved in your community and with your customers)

- Images & Videos

If you already have negative content out there, it must be either removed or suppressed. If the content cannot be removed, work on enhancing your online presence by focusing on promotional opportunities to highlight the good and mitigate the negative. One way to do this is by using strategic search engine optimization (SEO) tactics. Keep in mind, SEO campaigns can take up to 20 or more weeks to elicit results. Focus on creating consistent, positive, and high-quality content to diminish the effect of the negative content.

Net Promoter Score: What You Need to Know

As a business owner, you want to provide the best products and services to your customers. Your goal is not just to attain a healthy bottom line, but also achieve great satisfaction, which shows in reviews. And these reviews lead us to discuss digital marketing and the Net Promoter System.

You build trust and rapport, design products and provide services that you believe in, and constantly work to improve your offerings. This is the heart and core of your mission that marks your excellence.

But you won't always have raving reviews. And one dissatisfied customer can pull your score down.

The problem with customer satisfaction scores is that they rely too much on emotion. A customer who answers a survey right after a purchase can give a different score if he answers it after a week or month. Even how you write the questions and what kind of questions you ask can affect the replies and may prove useless in the end. And with a very long survey, the respondents tend to dwindle, giving you limited information.

To get more meaningful data, Fred Reichheld, with the help of the Bain Team and Satmetrix, developed a tool that can predict how customers would behave based on their satisfaction level.

What is the Net Promoter Score?

Reichheld would describe the Net Promoter Score as that one number that could predict business growth and customer loyalty. In an article he wrote for Harvard Business Review in 2003, "The One Number You Need to Grow," he revealed how Enterprise Rent-A-Car inspired this scoring system.

During a forum, Andy Taylor, then CEO of Enterprise, showcased his company's simple survey consisting of only two questions to measure customer loyalty:

How do the customers rate the quality of their rental experience? How likely are they to rent a car again?

The short survey had these advantages:

– It yielded a high response rate.

– The results were predictive of profits and growth.

– It identified the key driver of growth, i.e., the enthusiastic customers.

Reichheld decided to come up with only one question to measure customer loyalty that predicts growth and make it even simpler. But that one question did not come as fast and simple. It took him two years of research.

Why did it take so long to research the idea of customer ratings?

He realized that:

- Customer loyalty was more than retention rate. Some stick it out just because! Retention rate doesn't translate to growth.

- Customer loyalty could not be measured by customer satisfaction alone. Take Kmart for instance, he cites. Despite its great rating, it went bankrupt.

- Survey tools could be rigged. Plugging in questions that suggest the answers and veer the customers to reply positively could give a falsely high rating.

How Did He Come Up With That One Question?

With the help of Satmetrix, a software company that dealt with real-time data analytics, and the Bain team, who helped him design the Loyalty Acid Test comprising of 20 questions, that one question emerged by studying the behavior of more than 4,000 responders and linking their survey responses with actual referral and repeat purchase of the product. This question provided the best statistical correlation between emotion and action.

What Is That One Question?

"How likely is it that you would recommend our company/product/service to a friend or colleague?" This one question assesses customer loyalty that can predict business growth.

Hi John,

How's it going? We try not to bother you with too much chatter, but every once in a while, we like to find out how we're doing.

So on a scale from zero to ten, how likely are you to recommend ContentFirst.Marketing to a friend or colleague? (Just click the appropriate number below).

| 0 | 1 | 2 | 3 | 4 | 5 | 6 | 7 | 8 | 9 | 10 |

not at all likely   extremely likely

John Arnott
CEO
ContentFirst.Marketing
John@ContentFirst.Marketing
(800) 550-5701

But asking this question is not enough. For the data to become useful, they created the following scale:

10 – extremely likely to recommend

5 – neutral

0 – not at all likely

To his surprise, the customer referral and repurchase behaviors clustered into three, which he labeled as follows:

Promoters – those who gave a rating of 9 or 10; these loyal people promoted the business to their families and friends and brought in 80% of the referrals.

Passively satisfied – those who gave a rating of 7 or 8; these people are easily wooed away by the competitors.

Detractors – those who gave a rating of 0 to 6; these people badmouthed the business 80% of the time and brought down the morale of the employees as well as the reputation of the company.

Afterward, Reichheld and the team compared the percentage of promoters and detractors and came up with The Net Promoter Score.

% Promoters – % Detractors = Net Promoter Score

With further research and increasing his sample size, Reichheld and the team found a strong positive correlation between the net promoters and the company's growth rate in terms of revenue. That one question generated a useful predictive value that businesses could use.

Therefore, a company's goal is to have a positive net score, i.e., more promoters than detractors.

Does This Question Apply to All Industries?

Reichheld noted that there were some exemptions, such as:

- When the customers are mere end-users with no choice about the use of the service or product. For example, the use of a specific database software offered by companies to their employees. In this situation, asking the question is irrelevant.

- When one player dominates the industry

- When the company operates in a particular niche

In the above cases, it's better to ask the customers these two other questions:

"How strongly do you agree that company/product/service sets the standard for excellence in its industry?" "How strongly do you agree that company/product/service deserves your loyalty?"

But is asking that one question enough? How will the organization improve without knowing the reasons for the low rating? This is where the Net Promoter System comes in.

The Value of the Net Promoter System in Marketing

The Net Promoter System entails digging into the root cause of the low rating and asking the detractors more questions with one goal in mind: to address their issues and improve the system.

There are many ways to use the data:

- Use process and performance improvement approaches and tools such as Root Cause Analysis, Pareto Chart, Fishbone Diagram, and the like to address the detractors' issues

- Highlight and promote the promoters' reasons for their enthusiasm and use in marketing strategies (testimonies on your website landing page, for example)

- Analyze how to convert the passively-satisfied to a promoter through the Plan-Do-Study-Act method

Using the Net Promoter System is a useful but largely untapped tool. And as a tool, your marketing can use it to achieve high quality and drive growth.

The Secret to Glowing Online Reviews

In our digital world, your reputation is everything. A couple of bad reviews of your ice cream shop on Yelp, of your beauty salon on Google, or your consulting firm on Facebook can warn off new and old customers alike. You want to be proactive about getting the good reviews out there, and they won't always appear on their own without any action from you. Think about it – are you more likely to go to the trouble of leaving an online review without prompting if you have a good experience or a bad one?

If you want to encourage your customers to leave you a glowing review, here are your key steps.

Send Surveys

First, make sure you're sending customers a feedback survey after a completed sale or transaction. We love the Net Promoter Score system because the question is simple, as I discussed above. You can't find your Promoters unless you're proactively asking for feedback on a regular basis. Once you've received those scores, sort through and see if there are patterns in the Detractor category you can address.

Follow Up

Next, for the Promoters (anyone who rates you a 9 or 10), send a follow-up email asking them to leave you a review on your site of choice: TripAdvisor for travel and hospitality, LinkedIn for professional services, Yelp for certain businesses, etc. You don't want to ask those who give you a 2, because those aren't the reviews you want to encourage. It's crucial to be diligent about asking every single Promoter to leave you a review because usually, only about 5% of them will follow through. But those glowing reviews, if you accumulate enough of them, will steadily boost your reputation online and translate to even more sales.

Reach Out to the Promoters

Twice a year, you should also email those Promoters. After thanking them for their business and support, remind them that your business is built on referrals from people like them, and ask them to refer you to a friend. This isn't just about getting a referral, though those are always a welcome bonus. It also serves to remind them they had a great experience with you, and might even prompt them to make another purchase. An all-around win-win, if you ask us.

Exercise 11:

Do an assessment of the way your brand is seen online. This might be very obvious to you, if you've recently received negative press. But if you're not sure, start doing some research. Check all your relevant review sites, not just one, and see if you spot any trends in your feedback. If you don't already have Google Alerts set up for your company's name, do a Google search for your brand and see what you find. The internet is so massive these days that it's quite possible for some negative feedback to slide under your radar.

_____

_____

_____

_____

_____

_____

_____

_____

_____

_____

Chapter 12

BUILDING YOUR
ONLINE COMMUNITY

Your final step in getting measurable results from your marketing campaign can be a fun one: creating an online community around your brand. This step is a natural extension of the online presence we talked about in the beginning of the book. But it's more than just setting up a Facebook page for your brand and posting deals from time to time.

Building an online community for your brand is a content creation strategy for your social media - delivering content to engage your target audience authentically. Authenticity is an increasingly important quality of marketing - younger generations of consumers are especially wary of traditional advertising. And social media is a powerful way to show the authentic values and content of your company, with only a small monetary investment. Social media also provides a frequent reminder of your company and the products or services you offer, as your audience goes about their day. Unlike big billboards or pricey pay-per-click campaigns, creating a social media community is low-cost but big in results. Building a successful social media community does require time and thought, however.

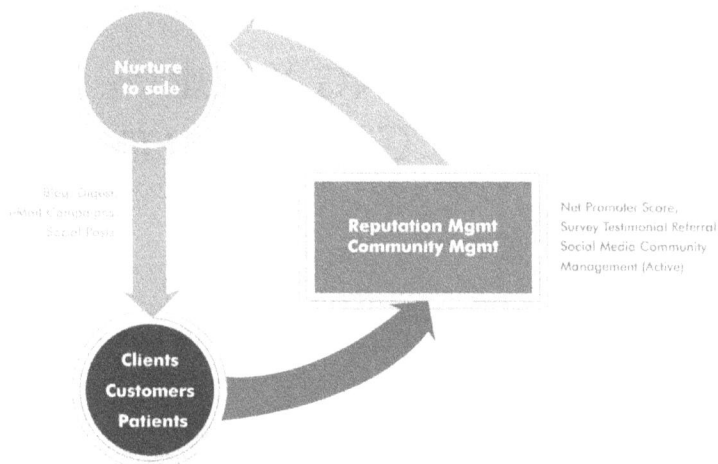

Social Media Management: Creating Authentic Engagement

As your online presence matures, thanks to your thoughtful hard work on the items above, you move from just posting content to managing a community on social media. This is an increasingly important component of staying engaged with your current and potential customers.

Keep Customers Engaged While Keeping a Good Reputation

This stage is about more than just trying to promote your business and creating general brand awareness. You need to engage your customers and your social media community. Ask questions, do surveys, share your customers' photos and thoughts, do giveaways – whatever is most likely to keep your audience authentically engaged.

Think of your online community as a way to build trust in your brand, and to remind your customers of your products and services on a regular basis without spending huge amounts on ad campaigns. Social media engagement helps separate your brand from the other similar services in the market - if you have a strong community of customers and prospects responding to your authentic content, you're already ahead of an over-saturated market.

Three Key Steps to Building Online Community

Start a Conversation

When you're considering what to add to your company's social media feed, don't just think about what looks good. Consider what kind of conversation it will create with your audience - will they feel engaged enough to comment or respond? The key to creating a community is conversations. Otherwise, it's just a one-way presence. Ask questions in your content, or share personal stories, or create polls and contests. A conversation goes both ways too - when your followers ask a question or comment, make sure you respond in a timely fashion.

Consider Your Target Audience

As I've discussed throughout the book, you don't want to waste your marketing dollars and valuable time speaking to a too-wide audience. This is even more important when building an online community - you bring them together because of a common issue or interest. Be sure your content speaks to your ideal customer - what they want, what they ask for, and what they keep coming back to discuss. It's better to have a smaller online community if it's a much more engaged one.

Encourage User-Generated Content

This is a step that pays big dividends for both your community engagement and your marketing budget. By encouraging your audience to create their own content where they are engaging with your brand or product, you get marketing content and a sense of ownership from your customers. If you're a shoe store, for example, you can ask your social media followers to post creative photos of themselves in your shoes on Fancy Feet Monday and share those on your channels. Your chosen pictures will delight the followers who created them, who are getting exposure to a wider audience, and you have authentic marketing created for you by your loyal customers.

Now that you have the general steps you need to take to build successful online communities, let's talk about some of the platforms you can use to launch your community. Facebook is the biggest and most general platform, and it might be the only one you think of when you consider social media. With more than 1.3 billion monthly users, Facebook is by far the world's most popular social media network. However, there are plenty of other social media networks that shouldn't be overlooked, as well. LinkedIn, Twitter, Pinterest, and Instagram are all powerful social media sites that business owners can use to promote their products and services. Instead of focusing your efforts strictly on Facebook, diversify and branch out into these smaller networks. But other options like LinkedIn and Instagram can pay big dividends for your business, depending on your audience. If you're trying to reach a younger audience or have a product with a strong visual component, Instagram is great. And if your target audience is professionals or businesses, LinkedIn can't be ignored.

Why Use LinkedIn for Digital Marketing?

Numbers don't lie - and they have steadily said that LinkedIn is one of the biggest social networks out there. At the end of 2019, there were over 610 million users, with steady growth each year. It's the largest social network exclusively for professionals. While other social networks like Facebook and Twitter are also popular, it's undeniable that LinkedIn is making a breakthrough.

When it comes to LinkedIn, you have a variety of ways to engage with customers. Here we'll break down some productive ways to connect with your audience.

1. Engage Groups

Joining industry-specific groups allows you to interact with customers and experts in your industry and take part in discussions by posting to group forums. This is a more natural and less self-promotional way to engage with your audience. It is an opportunity for you to show the human side of your organization, be conversational, ask questions, and weigh in on relevant discussions.

2. Write Influencer Posts

You can post original content stemming from your company's blog posts. If there was a popular article on your company's site, rework it into a more personal opinion piece to generate dialogue.

3. Create Showcase Pages

Showcase pages allow followers to subscribe to receive notifications when there are updates or new materials posted. You can use ads here to find leads who could benefit from your services.

4. Open Dialogue with New Contacts

Once you are connected with a new contact, you now have a platform to engage in dialogue. Send a quick thank-you note if they accepted your connection request or a short introduction if they added you. Follow up by offering to answer any questions they may have. You can even invite them to groups of which you are a part or sponsor on LinkedIn directly.

5. Curate Peer-Generated Resources

Many of our purchase decisions today are made after getting recommendations from friends or peers. After all, the consumer market today is vast and often overwhelming. LinkedIn is a great way to share knowledge and resources with your audience about issues they face. If you share through truly, it can make your target audience feel like you're a trusted authority who understands their needs. For example, if you own a technology consulting firm, you can share articles about tech trends and solutions from other authorities in the field, as well as your own helpful articles.

Why Use Instagram for Digital Marketing?

Instagram is a straightforward and visually engaging way to connect with prospects and tell your company's story. Use this platform to give a more personal look to your company and make existing customers and potential prospects feel more connected to you and your team. A little glimpse into your company could mean new customers.

1. Cover the Basics

If you're completely new to Instagram, there are a few items you need to take care of before going any further.

- Choose a catchy yet relevant profile name

- Use a high-quality image for your profile picture

- Search the right hashtags to include on your posts

- Complete the package by writing a bio that gives followers all the info they need – name, industry, location, and a link to your website.

2. Create Engaging Content

Now that your profile is ready to go, you can turn your focus to creating compelling content. High-quality images and videos are the only way to go. If you use poor quality images, people will stop viewing your profile.

Write clever captions and link to relevant users. For example, if you partner up with another company, consider featuring their page to connect followers. If you feel you don't have time to create quality content, you should plan it out ahead of time and use scheduling apps like Hootsuite to plan out content.

3. Introduce the Team

There's no better way to showcase your talent and introduce your voice than by using Instagram to create relationships. Do this by sharing photos of you and your staff with short intros. Or even do posts like "staff member of the month" (or week) depending on how large your company is and let customers form connections with your team.

4. Niche "Stuff"

Use your profile as a way to "geek out" and show customers what you're all about. Share pictures or videos of the latest equipment and trends. Whatever items are considered the cool content of your field will surely be a good post on Instagram.

You don't have to create all of the content for your social media accounts by hand. Nearly all of the leading social media networks allow users to share other users' content on their respective profiles and pages. Business owners should take advantage of this feature by sharing content that's relevant to their target audience. While uploading and using another person's image is usually a copyright violation, sharing content is not.

5. Customer Photos

Depending on your field, many customers are already sharing photos of their visits and purchases. Before-and-after shots are especially popular in some industries, such as hairdressing or cosmetics. Talk with your customers and see if they'd consent to being showcased on your brand's Instagram.

For example, take a page from the book of Instagram-famous dermatologist Dr. Pimple Popper (who garnered so much attention on Instagram that she now has a TV show).

Why Building a Community Matters

You want to be seen as a respected leader in your field, as a trusted and real brand, as an exciting and engaging company who's not afraid to get out there and be seen. This keeps your customers and prospects coming back to your social media or your website, keeping you in their minds as they go about their lives. With the amount of time most of us spend on social media these days, time spent on community management (or even the cost of dedicating a resource to spend time on it for you) is an investment with the potential for some big returns.

This long-term exposure all ties back into the nurture campaign as well – getting them primed to think well of you and your products while you nurture that relationship into an eventual sale, and from there into a long-term customer relationship. If you do this right, your customers will return again and again, back into the nurture funnel repeatedly without expensive ad campaigns. They come back because they feel genuinely connected to you, to your brand, and to what you're selling.

Exercise 12:

Take stock of your main social media presence - maybe it's Twitter, maybe it's Facebook or Instagram. Look through your last 10 posts for your brand. What was your engagement rate on those posts? Do you get many comments and see dialogue starting, or is it just some likes? This will tell you where you are in creating your online community. If you see dialogue happening, sharing going on, and lots of comments - great! If not, what are one or two things you could add to your posts going forward to start those conversations?

_____

_____

_____

_____

_____

_____

Chapter 13:

SUMMARY:
MEASURING THE RESULTS OF
YOUR MARKETING SPEND

In the last 12 chapters, I've shared all the knowledge you need to create a marketing plan that gets you measurable results on your budget. From creating a compelling online presence to generating and managing leads and nurturing them to a sale, we've covered it all together.

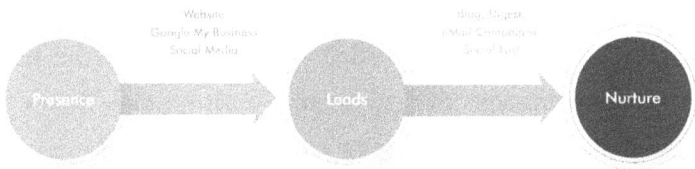

All of these steps are part of small cycles – the presence and the leads as one, the nurture, reputation, and community management as another. Ticking off a few linear steps can be great for getting one-off business but building your business over the long-term means thinking strategically over a few years, not a few months. You can hire a digital marketing company to help you with your marketing efforts, of course.

But with the right tools we've given you above, you can also craft a plan with a little thoughtful work. Digital marketing is one of the most cost-effective ways to market your business, whether you have a big, well-established business or are a brand-new startup.

After all, you built this business because you care about what you do and what you provide to your customers, not just about the bottom line. Your digital marketing strategy should reflect that care and that passion and create a way for your business to thrive for many years to come. Your digital marketing strategy really all boils down to the story you're telling about your business - who your customers are, what they need and want and deserve, what you offer to make their lives better. An effective strategy helps you tell that story in the places where your target audience is likeliest to hear it. And don't be afraid to get specific. You can't be everything to everyone, and if you try, you run the risk of diluting your message and connecting with no one. That's why you need to get specific and get strategic to see results.

Spending Thoughtfully

When it comes to promoting your business, it can be difficult to know which of the many marketing ideas is right for your business. The huge number of options available to small business owners is more of a blessing than anything else, though. It means that there's a tried-and-true marketing strategy out there that will work for businesses of any size.

Whether your business is just budding, and the marketing budget is small, or you're part of a larger company looking ahead to the next step, taking the time to research the options available to you is a step in the right direction. There's never been a better time to take advantage of digital marketing and all it has to offer.

The most effective digital marketing strategy is one that is comprehensive. It takes into account emerging trends and engages a number of different channels. It uses available data to inform its marketing tactics and offer its product or service to a large targeted audience. In turn, you'll see increased brand awareness, more qualified leads, and more customer engagement.

With consumers spending more and more of their time engaging with the digital world, there are few better investments for a company.

Results Come from Strategy

The one top tip I can give you for how to get results from your marketing dollars? Have a clear and defined marketing strategy. Waste often comes in when the overall strategy is unclear - when you're just trying things with no clear plan.

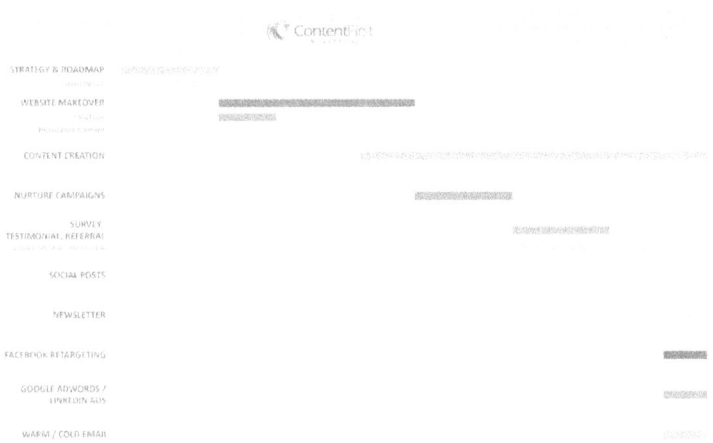

ContentFirst

STRATEGY & ROADMAP

WEBSITE MAKEOVER

CONTENT CREATION

NURTURE CAMPAIGNS

SURVEY
TESTIMONIAL, REFERRAL

SOCIAL POSTS

NEWSLETTER

FACEBOOK RETARGETING

GOOGLE ADWORDS /
LINKEDIN ADS

WARM / COLD EMAIL

Having a strategy in place - one that is based on research about your own industry - and a plan to measure the results allows you to focus on what's really working for your business. Looking at the data regularly is critical as well - digital marketing gives you plenty of info to dig into, but it won't help unless you make time to look at it. The digital marketing world changes quickly, and getting left behind can mean pouring money into avenues that aren't delivering for you. A regular review of your strategy and data will keep you up to date.

Results You Can Measure

When you partner with a digital marketing organization, such as ContentFirst.Marketing, make certain they have a philosophy and culture around measurement and optimization. What tools do they use? How can you monitor their efforts? ContentFirst. Marketing uses a custom developed portal called the C1M. app. This is specifically created so that each element of a digital marketing strategy can be measured. And, each question around the effort can be answered. Such as:

- What leads have arrived?

- What channels are driving the most leads?

- When someone calls the office, what experience does that lead receive?

- How are my email digests and campaigns performing?

- Is my site getting more traffic?

- Do my quick leads campaigns deliver leads within the framework of the lifetime value?

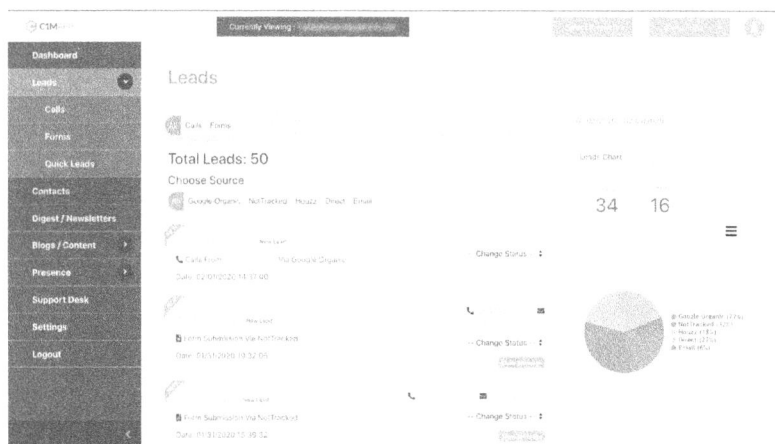

I hope you found the information in this book helpful, informative, and actionable. Creating ways for businesses to grow and build on their success is my passion, and I enjoyed sharing it with you. With the strategies in this book, you'll know exactly how successful your marketing campaigns are going when you implement them. I wish you great and measurable success.

Exercise 13:

Gather all your reflections from the previous exercises. That's your head start on your complete marketing strategy! It's time to come up with a complete one - feel free to redo any exercises as needed. Re-reading chapters can also be helpful if there are areas where your business needs more help.

Business owners are tired of spending their time and money on marketing efforts that don't deliver measurable business growth. At ContentFirst.Marketing, we use data and our years of expertise to help them avoid expensive mistakes and get results they can see and understand, delivering growth for the long-term.

In 2013, ContentFirst.Marketing was created with a clear mission – to help businesses grow.

With over 17 years of experience working with small businesses, the ContentFirst.Marketing cofounders know exactly what business owners need to for their companies to grow and thrive in today's marketplace.

We have been there. We know what it is like to build a business. We know how important it is to get marketing right.

We focus on real and measurable results, using techniques backed up by solid data. There's no guessing games or vanity metrics with us – just real growth you can see. And we partner with our clients to ensure they understand every component of what we do for them – from the website basics to strong content creation to increasing brand recognition.

Our mission is "Growing Businesses with Great Writing, Consistent Follow-up, and Measurable Results."

We always look at our work and ask, "Is this going to help this business grow?"

If you're looking for growth that positions your business for the long term, that gives you results you can measure and data you can understand, you need an expert team on your side.

You need ContentFirst.Marketing.

So visit us at http://ContentFirst.Marketing to schedule your free strategy call today, and get on the road to your own measurable results.

www.ingramcontent.com/pod-product-compliance
Lightning Source LLC
Chambersburg PA
CBHW071554200326
41519CB00021BB/6752